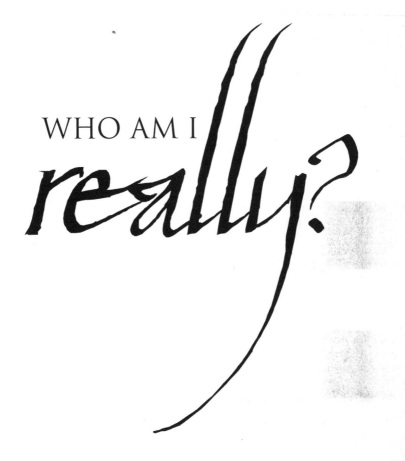

WHO AM I really?

THE AUTOBIOGRAPHY OF
ANNA ROSENBURG

AS TOLD TO KATHERINE MOORE COOPER

WHO AM I

really?

THE AUTOBIOGRAPHY OF

ANNA ROSENBURG

AS TOLD TO KATHERINE MOORE COOPER

Edited by Chris Newton

MEMOIRS

Cirencester

Published by Memoirs

MEMOIRS

Memoirs Books

25 Market Place, Cirencester, Gloucestershire, GL7 2NX
info@memoirsbooks.co.uk www.memoirsbooks.co.uk

ISBN 978-1-908223-35-7

Printed in England

Katherine Moore Cooper

I knew that when I met Anna that we had a connection that would unite us for the rest of our lives. Her spirit of life and her determination to live it to the fullest drew me into her world. Her story still moves me to this day.

The fact that Anna is a mother, a grandmother and a very respected woman in her community is a true testament to the love she experienced as a child. No one should ever have to endure what Anna has endured, yet she is a shining light to us all. She embodies the fact that we do not have to use our past hurts as excuses for bad behaviours but rather should use them to grow and make a better life for us and for those around us.

I would like to thank my husband Paul for putting up with me during the process of writing this book. My daughter Maya was born during the birth of Anna's story and the two of them will share a bond forever. I feel blessed that my daughter has such a remarkable woman as an adopted grandmother.

I must not neglect to mention the fact that I would not be writing anything if it had not been for my grandfather, Dr Tom M. Oliver. He made me see the power of words and the truth of friendship.

Katherine Moore Cooper

Dedication

I would like to dedicate this book to the following people: my Father Israel Rosenburg, known as Harry Ross, my daughter Ruth, my son Leo and my grandchildren Aaliyah and Maya.

Acknowledgments

Four years on and we've finally made it! Thank you Kat for dedicating the last four years to this project. Not only are you a talented writer, you are also an excellent listener. You've listened to my rants and ravings, you've watched me pacing up and down your house, you saw me laugh, you saw me cry and you calmly carried on. I feel blessed to have met you and know that I have found a friend for life.

Thank you 'big' Ruth for your friendship over the last 32 years. You of all people know me best and have been there for me through good times and bad, and I thank you for that.

Thank you Sarah, for coming into 'my world' and supporting me. You truly are a wonderful friend.

Thank you to Judy and Edward for helping me to get this kick started.

And last but definitely not least, thank you to my publishers Chris Newton and Tony Tingle. Chris for his incredible patience with me, emailing him constantly, and Tony for his brilliant artwork.

Finally I would like to say that I did not set out to offend anybody mentioned in this book.

Introduction

This book is about my life so far. However it is only a small part of the story, there's a lot more to me than what's written in this small book. I'd like to believe that although at times my life has been difficult, I am a well-balanced, happy human being.

Contents

CHAPTER ONE

"You have forgotten me!"

My life, until I was seven, was happy.

There was just my Dad and me. We lived in a basement flat in Camden Town. It was very small; there was just a front room where the cooker was and my bed, and a back bedroom where my dad used to sleep. We had no bathroom, just an outside toilet.

Twice a week we would go to the public bath and I would bathe. I used to love that. I would take my towel and my soap, and the lady there would run a huge bath for me and I would sit in it and wash and wash. And then the lady (I think her name was Mavis) would say, 'Come on Anna, come on, it's time to get out, hour's up my lovely!'

I would jump out and get dressed and feel all warm and clean. She always gave me a sweetie. 'Bye Anna!' she would say.

We had a neighbour, a smart lady called Janet who lived in a big house across the way. She was our friend and used to take me places and let me play at her house. She had a cottage in the country, and she used to take me there.

One day Janet said to me, 'Come on, Anna get ready! We're off to the country!' I remember her car; it was an Austin A40.

'Come on, Anna!' Get in!' she said. I got into the car, ready for an adventure in the country.

And then she said something very odd to me.

'Don't forget to bring Noname!'

Noname was my teddy bear. I thought it was strange, because I never took him with me. I always left him at home on my bed. And now she was telling me not to forget him. But I was a child, and used to doing what Janet told me to do.

I went to get Noname, put him in the car beside me and waved goodbye to my father. 'Bye–bye, Dad, bye–bye!' But when my father waved back to me, his face seemed to be wet. I remember he looked very sad. I thought to myself, 'it's because he's just shaved'. My dad shaved every day; maybe he still had water on his face.

That was that. Off I went with Janet in her car to go to her cottage, or so I thought.

As we were driving, I kept thinking it was a longer journey than I remembered from the last time. 'Should it be this long?' I kept asking myself.

When we arrived, it was a different place. 'This isn't the cottage!' I said.

It was a lovely place, with children everywhere. We had never been there before, but I was with Janet and she knew what I liked. 'Maybe I am here to play with other children' I thought. 'Maybe it's a special place!'

We got out of the car together and Janet took my hand. There was a long pathway that led to a big house. It crunched under my feet as we walked and I thought that was funny.

Janet knocked on the door and we went in. A lady said to me, 'Hello, you must be Anna.' I smiled and said, 'Yes, yes I am!'

She led us into a room. She and Janet were talking about something very important, I knew because they had their serious adult voices. I can't remember what they said, just lots of adult talk. Then the nice lady told me to go and wait in another room. They brought me a big glass of milk and a biscuit. This was a treat, so I sat down at the table and ate the biscuit and drank the milk.

No matter how hard I try, I cannot forget what happened then.

Janet and the smiley lady chatted and chatted. I sat with my milk and biscuits just listening, trying to understand what was happening. I heard the nice lady say, 'but she seems a happy child…and so well-nourished.' I wondered why she said I seemed happy. I was happy! There was more chatting. Then there was silence.

I went to the window. Janet was walking towards her car. Without me!

'Silly Janet, silly Janet, you've forgotten me!' I put the milk down and raced out, shouting for her. 'Janet! Janet! JANET! You've forgotten me!' I was now screaming as loudly as I could.

She got into her car and drove away without looking back at me once.

'Janet, you have forgotten me! Jaaaaaaanet! Janet, YOU HAVE FORGOTTEN ME!'

Someone was holding me down. I was shouting and screaming. 'Janet, you have forgotten me!' over and over again. Still they held me, and still I screamed.

The screams came from everywhere. I felt as if I was covered in a big thick black fog filled with screams. They came from the fog, from me, from every direction. I could not breathe. I was suffocating.

At last it went silent. Janet was gone and Dad was gone. I had only Noname. For days and weeks, I could not speak. The black fog would not leave me. And that was the beginning of it all.

CHAPTER TWO

Being different

In our world today, the news is full of reports of children in horrible abusive situations. Rarely do you hear stories about the ones who are saved, whose lives become average and normal again. Each of our elected governing bodies believes its way to save, to rescue, to keep from harm, is the right way.

Policies change and new legislation comes in to 'protect the children'. Everyone assumes that it will be good for a child to remove it from a situation which right-thinking people see as a 'problem'. But what if that removal was not done for the right reasons? What if it was for absolutely the wrong reason? The child is taken away from its home, its family and everything it knows. Children survive – that is what they do – but the scars of what we do to them live on.

I was one of those children. At seven years old, I was taken from the happy, secure environment of my home and put into care at a Barnardo's Children's Home. It happened more than half a century ago, yet the scars are still bright red and weeping from the inside.

Every day of my life I am affected by what happened to me. Every day of my life I wonder what would have happened if I had been allowed to stay with my father. I will never know.

I spent the rest of my childhood filled with anger at the world. I blamed all those I came into contact with for my sadness and my loss. The year I was 'removed' was 1957, long before government bodies were established to ensure the safety of children. The application for my admission to Barnardo's was made by the woman who lived across the street from me. The entrance papers were signed by her and my own father. She made him believe that it was the right thing, the best thing, the only way.

Janet Darlington was one of those people you meet in life who always has a project, something they need to fix. My little family became her project. In order to fix us she wielded her power and influence. She persuaded my father, a man on his own, poor and with only a basic education, that keeping me in a one-room basement flat was not the best thing for me. She convinced him that he was not fit to be my full-time parent. I never asked for her help, and I am sure my father didn't either.

My father was a simple man. He had had little education and came from a very humble background. Janet was rich and smart and knew things. He was obviously impressed by this woman from a completely different way of life who made him believe that raising a female child on his own in our simple little flat was somehow wrong.

I was born into a world that had just survived a devastating war. Britain was bruised and battered and reeling from the effects of losing an entire generation. There was no infrastructure in post-war Britain and the country was suffering from massive poverty. When I was born in 1949, Britain was a country that was still in the dark ages. Our class system had never been stronger.

If your place was in the working classes, you lived in conditions that by today's standards would be third world. That's how my father and I lived. We had one large room with a small scullery. We had running water but no bathroom, and we had to share a toilet. We were no different from our neighbours - everyone around us lived like that. Going to the public bath once a week was commonplace for many families, especially in the city of London.

The only thing that made us different was the colour of my skin.

My birth mother was a young Irishwoman who worked alongside my adoptive parents in Camden Market. She was married and already a mother to two children. I have been told that my birth father was a US soldier stationed in the UK, stationed here to help Britain re-structure after all of the devastation, and that he was black.

I will never know why my mother gave birth to me. Maybe abortion was not something she could afford or arrange, or perhaps she thought it was a sin. Maybe she thought she could pass me off as white; maybe she did not realise that the soldier was my father.

Whatever the reason, it was obvious as soon as I was born that I was not her husband's child. I will never know if she wanted me or not; whether or not she was sad, and cried when I was given up. I have so many questions about the adoption part of my life that will never be answered.

At three months old, I was adopted by a Jewish couple who worked in the market with my birth mother. My adopted mother and my birth mother were apparently friends. The Jewish couple who adopted me had recently lost twins at birth. Maybe they were recovering from the sadness of their loss and wanted a baby so badly that they did not care that I was black.

The fact remains that they wanted me and seemed not to be concerned about raising a black baby in a world where being black was a stain. I became their legal child, the daughter of Harry Ross (né Rosenburg - he changed it to avoid any anti-Semitism) and Selina Ross. For reasons I will never know, Selina left my father soon after I was adopted and Harry raised me the best way he knew how.

I grew up in Camden Town, where my father sold balloons and children's trinkets in the market. When he was not in the market, he was a tick-tack man – a bookie - at the races. My early childhood memories are completely happy ones. I remember perfectly our little basement flat. It had a bed, a cooker, a fire, and tiny windows that steamed up on Sundays when Dad made a Sunday roast.

Sundays were my favourite days. We would get up and take a walk, stopping at the local shop for the paper for him and comics for me, and then back to the flat for a roast dinner. It was a ritual for us, and I remember it vividly. I read the serialised Bunty and Judy comics and my father propped up his feet with the papers. The radio was always on and we listened to The Black and White Minstrel Show in the evening.

CHAPTER TWO

Silence

You know when we walk
And we don't even talk
Because there is nothing to say

And our hands are held tight
In the dead of the night
And the pain of the world goes away

Then you look down at me
And take in what you see
And accept me for who I am

Well, I'd just like to write
In the dead of this night
Try and remember one thing

That wherever we are
And whatever they do
They can never take me
Away from you.

It is important to make it clear that I was happy. I loved my father desperately. He never did anything to make me unhappy. In fact, it was just the opposite. The earliest memories I have are walks through Regent's Park and seeing glimpses of animals at the zoo. I can still see us gazing through bars at the zoo at the lions and tigers. I can hear the roar of the lion as I clasped my father's hand for safety. I can hear his footsteps next to me as we walked. I was safe in that city, with him at my side.

I attended a local primary school. Like every child of the time, I had my milk and cod-liver oil every day and took a long afternoon nap. Dad or my child-minder was always there to pick me up in the afternoon. We would go to the market and I could play around. I knew everyone and everyone knew me. I would run around with the other children getting sweeties from everyone. It was a true community, the kind that took care of its own. It was an idyllic way to grow up.

Sometimes, when Dad was at the races or working, I went to see a woman who lived across the road and looked after children. My memories of staying with her are happy, but then she was forced to stop looking after children by a concerned individual in the community; our neighbour, Janet Darlington. Across the road from our very working-class building were posh homes and flats, and Janet came from the other side of the road.

In 1956, when I was seven, Janet began to take an 'interest' in me. At first after the child minder was shut down she and my father had an arrangement - she would look after me instead. I have always wondered why a woman of her means and education would have cared about me. Maybe she felt sad that I had no mother; maybe she thought my 'vagabond' existence was not right. Whatever her motivation, it was clear that she believed she would 'make a difference'. She certainly did that.

Janet was originally from the USA. Rich and well educated, she married a middle-class educated British man and came to live in London, across the street from us. She moved in the circles of the intellectual élite. She and her friends wanted to change the ways of the British 'poor' and our 'filthy' living conditions. Their altruistic ideals were directed towards me. I was the beautiful little brown girl across the road, motherless and poor, a perfect subject.

Janet became a foster mother to me. To try to educate me and show me a different side of life, she took me to places with her and her family. We went to the countryside, to their weekend cottage in Suffolk. I was expected to attend dinner at her house and sit at the big table with her smart friends, listening and absorbing their ways - how they ate, what they ate, how they spoke, what they said. There were politicians, architects, writers, and professors. From the beginning, it seemed normal. Kids are very adaptable. Afterward, I would go back to my basement flat and resume my regular life with my father, warm, loved and happy.

Janet commented often on how clever I was, and that made me proud. I tried so hard to please her. My outward appearance was appreciated as well. I had skin the colour of coffee and big, wide, smiling eyes. I loved being with her - she was a mother figure when I had no mother of my own. Her home offered a very different alternative to mine. There were lovely books to read, trips to the cottage, beautiful gardens to play in and interesting new food to eat. Her house was enormous, and sparkling. The garden was all hers, and perfectly maintained. To have your own private garden in London right behind your home was something no one I knew would ever have, but Janet had it.

The whole family was kind to me; her husband, Tom, and her son Edward welcomed me with open arms. I even had my own room - in their town home and in the country cottage. I wonder what my father thought of it all. Was he happy to have some time to himself and not have to worry about who was looking after me? Janet must have impressed him. He must have had complete and utter trust in her to let me spend so much time with them.

When she told me we were going to her cottage, it was not an issue; it was something very normal in my life. I trusted her as I would have trusted a mother. I never imagined that she could do what she did, that she would abandon me at Barnardo's on that fateful day.

'No Destitute Child Ever Refused Admission' was the motto of Barnardo's Homes for Destitute Children. It was all the idea of Dr Thomas Barnardo, back in the Victorian era. The first homes were built to house the thousands of orphans living in the streets of London. Cholera and typhoid were rampant after the Industrial Revolution and Dr Barnardo became the orphan's champion. He died in 1905, but his charity was well established by then and by the time of his death, there were over 90 of his homes. After World War II the displaced children of Britain became a national problem, and Barnardo's led the way towards helping. Barnardo's became a very successful charity organisation and a place for children to have a safe, healthy environment in which to grow up. It was not an orphanage or a workhouse but a place of refuge, offering warmth, food, health and security.

Yet I already had warmth. I had a home and food and went to school. I had a father who loved me and whom I loved. We did not live on the streets and we were not destitute. That did not stop me ending up a Barnardo's child.

★ ★ ★ ★ ★ ★ ★ ★ ★ ★

May 2008: a letter drops through the letterbox. As I hear it drop I already know its contents. I have been waiting a year, or rather, a lifetime.

It is a large envelope, heavy with importance. I put it on the table. I do not tear it open; it can wait a little longer. Coffee is made and still the letter waits. It is not junk mail, or a bill, or a notification. It is official; it is important. It shouts out 'look at me!'

I pick it up to silence it. I stare and stare at it.

The image of all I knew before comes into my mind. I smell the musky smell of our flat. I see the old scullery, with my father doing the washing up. I feel the heat of the little fire on my face. I smell the lingering smell of a Sunday roast, the same smell that fills my own kitchen years later. My windows fog up with steam and I can see his hand, his long brown fingers drawing funny cartoons in the wet steam. I laugh out loud.

But I am no longer that child. I am a grown woman with children of my own. Today, maybe, the answers to some of my questions are in that envelope.

I pick it up and open it. Slowly, I take the contents out; a sheaf of A4 paper. My hands shake. This document controls me; its contents have controlled my whole life. This stack of paper is all I have of my life after the basement flat.

I read and read. And then I cry. What else can I do?

My time at Barnardo's is all sketches and memories. Until May 2008, those memories were all the evidence I had. In 2000 the Freedom of Information Act was passed and I could finally ask Barnardo's to send me the paperwork they had on me.

I waited over a year to get it. Waiting for it became part of my life, and it made me angry at the 'system'. The paperwork was my life. It was the reflection of all my years in the home. Yet to be allowed to see it, I still had to prove who I was; wait; wait some more; have counselling for what I was about to receive; wait some more; and then, fall back to the end of the line because I was not at the end of my life. This whole period felt as if Barnado's still controlled me and every aspect of my life.

But then, finally, it came through the letterbox.

The first pages were dated from the time just before I was admitted to Barnardo's to the day I became an adult in the eyes of the state at 21 years old. Fourteen years of a life, my life, packed into an A4-size brown envelope. My main growing-up experience was a series of medical examinations, yearly checkups, disciplinary records and social workers' reports. It was all there – my early life in black and white.

The most shocking thing to me was seeing my father's signature on the admission papers. Janet Darlington's signature was right next to his. You could see her strong letters directing his less decisive scrawl to the page. Her influence over him was clear in every confident stroke.

Seeing his name on the admission papers was hard for me to take. The realisation that he had condoned all this and allowed me to be taken away hit me with full force. There was no way either of them could fully understand the psychological impact their act would have on me. They did not set out to damage me, only to try and help me. I know that now.

I felt a strange connection to him again. Seeing his signature was like seeing his big brown tobacco-stained hand take mine. But he was not the one who took me away, it was not he who left me all alone in a children's home with nothing but my teddy. No, that was Janet.

My principal 'application for admission' papers to the Barnardos' home at Barkingside show me to be a healthy child of average weight and health, who attended school. The papers are third party applications, but the tone of the person who filled them in is evident. They refer to my adoptive father as a person of 'good character, but not stable - a gambler.' Although he had a home and a job and was in relatively good health.

On every page I am referred to as a 'half-caste child' or 'coloured'. This was striking, considering the modern-day ideology of race and its terminology, but of course this was the mid 1950s and it was a totally different time.

The papers also revealed that it was Janet Darlington and the local health visitor who presented me to Barnardo's for admission. It was their idea that I was not receiving 'proper' care living with my father; this proved to me, once again, how heavily he was being influenced by Janet and the authorities.

Strangely, there are some papers that show I was being 'watched' by a local social worker before my admission to Barnardo's. The pages also reveal that my father was paying certain women in the neighbourhood to look after and care for me, the primary one being Janet Darlington. I do remember my father working most of the week.

The paperwork reveals that my father had used many different options for child care. The tone of the writer, the social worker, conveys a sense of worry about this and indicates that it was not good for me. It says: 'Candidate (me) undoubtedly lacks security, having had so many changes. Adoptive father has had a series of housekeepers and daily minders for candidate and she has had at least 3 foster mothers in the last 18 months.'

The writer also reveals that my father was starting to go to hospital to be treated for varicose veins and that this was stopping him from earning enough cash to pay for my care. I was struck by the line 'if he decides to let her go into our care, when in employment he would willingly pay £2-10-0 pw.' It is hard to swallow this fact - my father actually contemplated letting me go into Barnardo's and paying for my care. As I read through the documents, I kept flashing back to the papers signing me in and his weak signature, so dominated by Janet's. I can't imagine what it was like for him to have all the social workers monitoring me as well as Janet.

My life was in that envelope. I was being discussed as if I were a lab experiment - watched and prodded, checked and re-checked. Not once did anyone think to ask what I would have wanted. No one asked me if I wanted to go to Barnardo's; no one asked me if I wanted to leave my father. My candidacy was discussed long before I was abandoned there. Yet I was seven years old, old enough for someone to talk to me and see if I minded different child-minders, or a life not filled with a routine. Because I can tell you, I didn't mind at all. I loved my life. Intellectually, I know that one doesn't usually consult a seven-year-old child about make life-changing decisions for themselves, but now I am screaming at them to ask me. I would have said 'NO! I WANT TO STAY WITH MY FATHER!'

The paperwork includes standard check forms - health, weight, appearance and attitude. The most unnerving thing about the entire stack is the reference to my past before I was adopted and to the adoption itself. It is not followed up, and nothing is revealed to allow anyone to know the truth. This is me! This is my history! It defines the first fourteen years of my life. It is all I have in writing to confirm my childhood memories.

I know that my adoptive mother and father knew my birth mother; I know my birth mother was white and already married. I know my birth mother was of 'low grade mentality' and that my natural father was a 'better type of coloured man'. While most people in the world have their whole family histories told to them all the time, I have admission papers from Barnardo's. Every adopted person I have ever met has expressed a desire or at least a curiosity about their natural family. I have to admit that I was hoping the paperwork would have revealed a clearer link to my genetic past.

One of the worst things about being adopted is visiting a doctor, as everyone must at some point in their life. I try to avoid new doctors, as they always ask about your family history. 'On your mother's side, any history of heart disease? What about diabetes? Do you know if any person on your father's side had cancer? Did your father suffer from sickle cell anaemia? Did your mother have high blood pressure?' Imagine what it is like to have to sit there and say, 'I don't know. I was adopted'. Over and over again.

I wish the paperwork had some answers. 'Have you tried searching for your family?' That question makes me want to scream and shout. Of course I have tried! And I wanted the paperwork to tell me, but the people who knew were not interviewed; no one went to the authorities and took my original birth certificate. No one asked my birth mother about my father. No one knows, so I don't know either, and I never will.

Being adopted is different for different people. I'm happy to hear of modern adoptions in which the child is told from the beginning who their parents are; sometimes they stay in contact. That amazes me.

Hearing about people who have found their families makes me sad and angry at the same time. These 'friends' are very happy to tell me of others' triumphs at finding out their history. Don't they realise how it hurts me to hear about it?

In the same vein, I do not want to talk to other adopted people and hear their stories of success at finding their families. I cannot have any more false hope. I will never know where my black skin comes from. I know my mother had two sons before I was born and may have had more children after me – I will never know. I know my brothers exist, I know they are out there somewhere, but too much time has passed and it has all been forgotten. My story is very different from other adoption stories. The hope that the paperwork might shed some light on my skin, was just that – a hope.

The greatest blow was that there was not one reference to my natural father. There was only the strange, unsubstantiated statement that he was a 'better type of coloured man'.

I still hold in my heart the story my adoptive father told me – my natural father was a black US serviceman stationed in London after the war. This minute detail has had the greatest impact on me, throughout my life. My whole life has been dominated by the colour he gave me. I am boxed and ticked as 'coloured', yet I have no idea of the true nature of that colour. Were his family from the Caribbean, or from Africa? Were they of slave descent in the USA? Did he suffer as much from prejudice as I have in my life?

I am a black woman who does not know the history of her own colour. I did not have proud grandparents with deep, cracked black skin to hold my hand and tell me how hard it will be to be black. I had no father to watch and imitate as he held up his black head through his life. I did not know how to be black and proud. I have been black and alone. And for that, I will always be lost.

It was when I was in Barnardo's that I first fully realised that my skin was black. I was ten or eleven, and I tried, desperately, to scrub the black off my skin. I scrubbed so hard I wounded myself. The urge to fit in was so strong that I was willing to self-harm.

Of course, I learned on my own. I had to. I learned how to hold my own head up high, how to walk into an all-white room and not cringe outwardly with stares and comments about my skin. I believe I managed it all with a grace and dignity which must have come from somewhere. But where? I will truly never know.

CHAPTER THREE

"A jolly little coloured girl"

The papers reveal so many things about me, confirming some of my memories though failing to document many more. I was described in a wide variety of ways, from being 'a jolly little coloured girl' to being 'spiteful to others'.

I wanted answers to my past to leap out from these copies, this paperwork from 50 years ago. Instead, I am left with more questions. All I had of my first year in care was the initial entry pages (still a shock), the background paperwork revealing I was being watched and the first medical reviews of my health. Then nothing.

I wanted to see the blackness and the deep profound sadness I experienced that first year documented. It's disturbing to know that this was not a concern for the Barnardo's staff. Maybe it was so commonplace that they simply disregarded it? I distinctly remember not speaking and not wanting anyone to speak to me. I remember black rages and fits of extreme anger. But there was no page of evidence for this anger. It's as if it never happened. It feels as if Barnardo's wanted to cover up my pain by not acknowledging it.

After a year, the documents reveal me to be a happy child, on the whole. Apparently, I wanted to play with others and share toys. My father came to visit every fortnight, bringing toys and sweeties. Dad also paid for my care, which I still find hard to take. He paid in advance; in fact, he was in credit. It makes me wonder why he couldn't use that money to keep me with him. There are no answers to that. But, to me, it proves that he felt powerless against more educated people making decisions for me.

Was I only acting happy for my dad, so that he wouldn't be sad like me? I know he must have been relieved to know that I was safe and well cared for. Once again – I will never know.

The documents included several reports through the years from one of my 'matrons', or aunties, as we called them. The first I read was from Auntie Scales; All I remembered of her was her hatred towards me. She stole my packages from my father and gave my sweets and biscuits to her favourite children, leaving nothing for me. Her report reflecting her feelings towards me, describing me as 'bad-tempered, moody, spiteful with other children'. This is the only paperwork written with this tone. I wish I could reach through time, grab her, shake her and scream 'leave me alone!' How dare she take away my packages, knowing they were my only link to the man I loved!

Yet the papers have some good in them. I was described as an honest little girl who was clean and tidy with a kind nature. I was left confused by my father's visits and the documents reveal that I was always upset after he left, but he never stopped coming to see me. Our relationship was described as loving and devoted. My memory of pure love from him is documented. It existed; it cannot be taken away. And that is a good feeling.

As with any large organisation, Barnardo's had rules and regulations. All children have to be fed, educated and taught a work ethic. I had tasks to perform and school to attend. We had to go to church every Sunday, regardless of our own religious background.

All the children had to adhere to Barnardo's basic principles, the main one being that there was to be no individuality. We were given clothes to wear, with heavy brown lace-up shoes forced on us. Most personal items were taken away. The only thing I was allowed to keep was Noname, my teddy bear.

It was impossible to understand this absence of personal attention – there were no explanations as to why. We must receive no individual attention, nor could any love be shown to any of us, although I had come from a home where I was loved. Each child had to conform to the Barnardo's way of life, to the Barnardo's 'family'. Maybe the other children were used to the loss of innocence. Perhaps they were happy that they were off the streets, or away from abusive homes. But for me, a lost, seven-year-old girl, it was all a huge shock.

There are only three pieces of paperwork from my first two and half years in Barnardo's. The first is a report from the social worker who had been watching me before my placement. She reports on a visit to our flat to check on my father's status. As he was paying for my stay, she wanted to ascertain if he might want to take me out in the future. She wanted to check his financial status.

Reading this made me so sad. But the funny thing about the report is her description of him. 'Adoptive father is an unusual type of man with whom one has to be tactful. He is a likeable man in many respects and his conversation and demeanour to me was all that it could be, but he has somewhat of a 'rough' "Cockney" background and could be a nasty customer on occasions.' When reading those lines, my heart swelled with pride. Of course he was a rough Cockney - that was where he was from! That was his world. How did they expect him to act?

There was also the reference to the fact that he did visit me and wanted to bring me a Christmas present- something I had asked for, a nurse's uniform. He obviously loved me so. He wanted me back. But I am sure that the social workers, Janet and the rest of the people who were 'interested' in me, thought he was too common, too rough, not stable. It makes me laugh. Today my situation would have never been looked at twice. I wasn't abused. My father paid for me to be looked after. I went to school. I was well fed, and loved.

His first visits to me were so painful. I couldn't understand why I couldn't leave with him and run back to our basement flat and hide away. Why did I have to stay? I would run after him, crying through the gates for him to take me home. I saw tears on his face too. It was too much to take. I know that he loved me.

I know my memories of his visits with sweets and gifts were not fantasies. He wanted to bring me a Christmas present. And that was the wonderful thing about reading my life in black and white, I knew that he had loved me, adored me, wanted me to be happy. He was somehow convinced that my being in Barnardo's was the right thing for me.

The only other papers from my first two years were the standard 'REPORT UPON CHILD.' These cropped up every year and basically reported on my so-called 'progress'. They have all the basic general information, health, school, contact with others, etc.

During the first two years I was healthy, a good reader, bright, but a bed wetter. However, the concluding comments almost always describe me as a bad mixer and spiteful to the other children. But the description that stands out is 'insecure and needing a lot of attention'. What did they expect? A child is removed from her home, taken from her father, whom she loves and placed in an institution in which she received no love, warmth or individual attention. Of course I was insecure and needed some attention! It is hard not to shout at the walls in defence of my little seven-year-old self.

During those first few years, I remember the visits from my father stopping for a while, I don't know exactly why. There is nothing in the paperwork to support this memory; there is nothing from the first year but the two reports. I believe his visits were just too traumatic for both of us. I distinctly remember his face swimming in tears as he turned to wave goodbye to me that first awful day.

At some point in my first few years, I was placed in one of the cottages for problem children, a rehabilitation unit. I was disruptive and mean to the other children because, I think, I was confused about my situation. The rehabilitation unit served to mould the child to accept the situation and become compliant. I would never be 'rehabilitated' so I remained in the 'problem children' cottages for the remainder of my stay.

For some reason, it was also home to all the kids who were different, mentally challenged and with physical disabilities. It was the harshest of environments, and at the time I had no idea why I was being forced to live there. It felt like a punishment. I did what any spirited, confident child would have done - I rebelled. I have never stopped rebelling. I knew I did not belong there. Even in my seven-year-old mind I could feel the injustice of it all.

All the children had duties and jobs to perform, and I was no exception.

The one I dreaded most was filling the coke bins with coal. At 5.30 every morning, in the dark, I had to walk down into the basement, with no light, and fill the bins. It was a horrific experience for me. The dark brought out my worst fears. But there was no way to get out of the job. The bins were very big and heavy and I could not run with them through the achingly cold blackness.

We all had to take the jobs in turn. I sometimes felt that I was being given the worst jobs because I had been labelled as a bad child. I always seemed to get either the coal bins or the other job I hated, cleaning the shoes of all the children in the cottage - 12 children, 24 shoes. Sundays were the worst, because I had to clean the Sunday-best shoes as well. 48 shoes to clean before church!

At other times I was on bathroom and bed duty or kitchen clean-up, but it was that walk through the cold, black basement for the coal that still keeps me awake at night.

Barnardo's had so many children to keep in order that they had to be very strict. To my child's mind, it seemed so cruel, and to my adult mind, my trained carer's mind, it still seems cruel. Why would you label a child a 'bad child', put them in the rehabilitation unit and keep them there? My adult self knows that my little-girl self was only reacting to the circumstances.

My paperwork also makes reference to my bed wetting. It seems that it was a problem I had on admission, but as far as I remember it began at Barnardo's. Wetting the bed was seen as bad behaviour, as if I was doing it on purpose.

My punishment was horrendous. Each morning after it happened I had to march across the grounds with my wet bedding to the laundry room, in front of all the other children, who would be laughing and pointing at me. Then, after the school day was over, I had to go back to the laundry room to retrieve my fresh linens. Not one person ever tried to comfort me or find out why I was wetting the bed. Imagine how it was for me trying to be friends with these kids who made fun of me all the time. It only made me stand out even more.

Because of my bad behaviour I was rarely allowed free time at the weekend, while all the other children were playing and riding the few bicycles we shared. When I was good, I could play with the other children and ride the green scooter that my father had given to me. But my scooter was used by all the other children too, and it was denied to me when I was 'naughty'. It was cruel.

While the others had their fun, I was made to scrub and clean the areas in and around Colonel Atkins' house. He was in charge of our home, which was one of the largest. I do remember him being kind to me. He had a large mosaic hallway in his home which I was forced to clean and he would chat to me about all sorts of things while I scrubbed away at the tiles. He ran a tight ship at the home, but he and his wife gave me attention and made me feel as if I was a little bit special. In fact I think I was deliberately naughty sometimes just so that I would be sent to see them. They were the only adults in my childhood – besides my father of course – who I can remember being kind to me and showing me love or attention.

At Barnardo's we were sheltered from the rest of the world. We had no concept of money and we all wore the same clothes and ate the same things. We played the same games, and our supplies were ordered by the matrons. There was no TV, no radio, virtually no link to the outside world. The only entertainment we were allowed was Songs of Praise on a Sunday in the matron's sitting room.

The only outside contact we had was the annual trip to Margate. One or two of the cottages went together on two big buses and spent two weeks at the seaside. It was bliss, and I will never forget it as long as I live. Camping in a local church, running wild on the beaches, the sun and sand – they were all such novelties to us.

At Barnardo's each child was assigned a cottage in which to live. I was sent to several before landing in the one for troubled children. Now, as a trained carer myself and a mother of two, I can see that my so-called 'rages' towards other children were only the result of the neglect and mean-spiritedness of the vindictive 'auntie' of my cottage. Her favourites got my packages and ate the things meant for me right in front of me.

Once one of the favourite girls took the last of the peas at dinner, and I became so angry that I pulled out her hair and left a bald patch. The auntie, Miss Toad – that was her real name! - hit me across the face so hard I got a black eye. Admittedly, it is the only memory I have of hand-to-body punishment at Barnado's, though we were caned in class, as was the rule of the day. But none of this is documented - only my mean-spiritedness towards the other children.

I was moved to another cottage, and another, and another. None of the other matrons could handle me. At the age of 10, I was moved to a cottage with a male 'matron', someone who could handle my physical attacks. This seemed to stop my rages somewhat, but I never really settled.

I stayed in this cottage for a while. The rest of the children stayed in the same cottages until they were ready to leave Barnardo's, which gave them a connection to other kids and matrons. I never had any connection to other children or to one particular matron, but there was a silver lining to all of this. Barnardo's policy of putting all types of children in their 'rehabilitation' cottages was very good for me. 'Rehabilitation' meant that the group of children were different - other black children, diabetics, disabled, children with learning difficulties, children with mental health issues, as well as 'normal' children. It was a good policy, and it turned out to be very good for me.

Eventually, after the male matron found ways to control my outbursts, I moved back in with Auntie Ann at Heather Rehabilitation Cottage. I stayed there until I left Barnado's. All the children, whatever their reasons for being 'rehabilitated', were together, and physical difference did not matter. From the beginning of my life I thought that was the way of the world; all types of people just lived together. And to be fair, this experience has enabled me to understand everyone's disabilities and physical and mental drawbacks in life. I connect completely with those who are labelled by society as 'different'.

Barnardo's was like a small village in and of itself. It was the largest home in the country, with 600 children and 60 cottages. There was a shop, a school, a church and a hospital, all on site. All the children who were sick were taken to the hospital. I used to sneak up to dance and play with the sick children through the window. I was never one of the sick children, but I always felt the need to go and see those who were.

I was a bit of a loner and did not have many friends, but I remember one boy, John, who had hydrocephalus. I would sneak over to the hill just under his window and chat with him, just to cheer him up. Then one day, he just wasn't there. He had died. And that is how it was. Some of the children simply died. It did not make me sad; it was just the way our life was. Barnardo's was run with no emotion, no love, no mothering at all. Hence, we were not introduced to the concept of mourning. I had to accept John's death and get on with my life.

The main school for Barnardo's was on the site, and every child under 13 went there. I was switched from class to class because of my attitude and behaviour, and I ended up in a class with much younger children. Although the minimal paperwork reveals me to be an adequate student, my memories are of being ostracised in class, for a variety of reasons. First, I was left-handed, which caused many problems. There were no special desks for the left-handed, so I had to sit at a desk which made it almost impossible for me to write legibly. Second, I am dyslexic, which made me stand out even more. Although I loved to read to myself, reading out loud was always hard for me. There was no special class for me or tutoring, just the label that I was 'difficult.' The many problems of school made me hesitant to want to learn anything.

My teacher, Mr Feather, was not one to spare the rod, and he often used to cane me. One day he caned me so hard that I cursed him like a witch and told him he was going to die. I can't remember why I said these things, or even more to the point, where the idea of cursing came from. But horrifically, the very afternoon of the caning, Mr Feather was killed on his bicycle riding home.

This had a profound effect on me. My guilt was horrible. The other children shunned me even more, as they thought of me as a witch who could curse people to death. Even the staff were afraid of me. I was now completely ostracised.

With everyone shunning me and the feelings I was having about myself, I fell into an even deeper sadness. It seemed nothing could make me happy.

Weekends with Dad

The paperwork reveals that on January 12, 1960, three years after I had begun living at Barnardo's, my father made an application for me to come home for long weekends and school holidays. This was the proof I needed that he never stopped loving me. He wanted me home at weekends!

The tone of the follow-up paperwork suggests that his request was not well received by my assigned social worker. She visited him in the flat and reported that it was 'still filthy and unfit for a child.' The subsequent paperwork reports that he cleaned it up and made it habitable for me. According to the report, there was a new landlord who had refurbished the building and found new tenants for the flats above us. My father showed the social worker a receipt for a new bed and bed linen for me. Now those long weekends at Barnardo's that were filled with chores and church would be replaced every fortnight by weekends in Camden Town with my father!

It took a good hour and a half to get from Barkingside to Camden Town. I remember the journey exactly; I will never forget it. Nothing changed from our old routine. I walked in Camden Market, chatting with the other vendors and running little errands for them, getting cups of tea and sweets. Everyone knew me, and I knew everyone. I was home and I was happy.

I can shut my eyes even now and see my father walking through the market, looking smart in his trilby hat and corduroy jacket. I can see him lifting his hat off, running his big strong hands through his hair and winking at me.

Sundays were the best - papers, comics, roast dinners and radio. Sometimes we went for a walk, sometimes we just stayed in; nothing mattered except us being together.

I always had to leave by three or four o'clock to make it back to Barnardo's by night fall; it was even earlier in the winter. It was a hard journey in the winter - very long and very cold. I never let my father walk with me to the train station. It was very difficult not to have those last moments with him, but I somehow knew I should not make a fuss.

I saw my father as much as they would let me. The man at the railway station remembered me - he called me 'Sunny'. Those visits to Camden were my salvation, but they also made me stand out even more from the other kids. I had a family, someone who loved me, someone to buy me sweets and cook me a roast dinner on Sunday.

I did not care what they thought; I longed even more for home. When I walked through the market, the vendors shouted my name and the women in the street said hello and welcomed me back. I knew everyone in the streets around me. No one in Camden thought of me as badly behaved or hard to handle. For them, I always had a smile and time for a quick laugh. Going back on Sundays to Barnardo's was like having my heart pulled out.

The funny thing that happened after my father petitioned to see me was that I started to see Janet again too. At that time in my life she still represented the only mother figure I would ever have, and I relished any attention she showed to me. As a child I could not make the association between Janet and my removal from my home. I do now, as an adult, and I hate her for it. But back then, I longed for anyone who knew me. Janet knew me, and our strange life resumed.

I would pop over to see her for dinner or a chat. Tom, her husband, was very nice to me and I liked playing with their son, Edward. I can remember many afternoons in Janet's beautiful garden. But for a young girl, it was so confusing. I lived in Barnardo's like an orphan, but I had a loving father and a mother figure too.

I'm confused, are you?

They say that I'm not like them
They say I'm not the same
They say I tried to fool them and play some silly game

They say they really hate me, and I say that's really fine
They say they didn't mean it
And I say I didn't mind

They say they're 'oh so sorry', and I say 'that's OK'
The say they get confused and mad
Well I knew that anyway

So, they came to an arrangement that I should go away
I turned my back and left them
Then they asked me 'would I stay?'

By now I felt confused and sad – they said they felt the same
I said that you don't know me
Then they asked me, 'what's your name?'
I said I did not have one and they said 'but you must!'
I said I'm not like them
They said 'you are one of us'.

So they came to an arrangement that I should go away.
I turned around and said to them
'I really want to stay.'

Looking back now with the 20/20 vision of hindsight I can see what I was to her – just a little coloured girl, her project. She could show me off to all her intellectual friends, making her look like a good-hearted, kind woman taking a interest in her community by trying to teach me a better way of life.

I was invited to dine with her houseguests. I even adapted my accent to the well-tuned ears of the middle classes who came to visit. Janet taught me to use the right utensils and made me eat strange and exotic foods (I still cannot eat an avocado!). I behaved like a proper middle-class girl at her dinner parties and around her friends.

She was training me well, but she also had me cleaning her toilets and dusting and mopping her floors like a servant. I wanted so much to please Janet, to hear kind words and feel some sort of motherly love, that I did everything she asked of me, without question. There was no love from her at all. She was cold, almost sterile, to all around her. She never said anything resembling a term of endearment. But I kept on trying. I never stopped wanting her to be like a mother to me.

It was a schizophrenic life. During the week, I was in care at Barnardo's. My weekends were divided between roaming Camden Market with my father and the posh world of Janet Darlington. It was all I knew.

Today I am equally at home at dinner parties and in the streets. I can switch on a posh accent at will. My mind can determine in an instant which side to show to the world. I can fit anywhere, but I still feel I fit nowhere.

It was during the first few months of visits home to Camden that I first discovered something which would become the one true love of my life. When I had my free time at Barnardo's I would wander around the grounds on my own. I was never missed at playtime, and it was quite easy to slip away.

There was a large forest near the grounds that drew my attention. One day, after making my escape, I came upon a group of travellers in the wood. They had appeared magically overnight. With them was a large black and white horse, and I was fascinated by it. Every chance I got, I sneaked away and watched the gypsies silently through their makeshift gates, secretly wanting to ride that wonderful animal.

The day finally came when they offered me a ride. I was given a rope halter, placed on the horse bareback, and off I went. I was hooked. After that, I went to see them as often I as I could get away for about five or six months, taking the big horse riding through the forest all alone. It was just me, the horse and the trees; I was left completely alone and at peace.

Then one day I went for my ride as usual and found the camp desolate and empty and the travellers gone. That's what travellers do of course, they just take off. Perhaps they were moved on by the powers that be, or perhaps they just felt it was time for a change of scenery.

I cried my heart out. I like to think that if they had known where I came from or how to get in touch, they would have said goodbye; in fact I am sure they would. But they never asked me any questions. They had no idea I was from Barnardo's, so they couldn't have sent a message. It was truly devastating. But it did leave me with a life-long love of riding horses.

One weekend I mentioned to Janet that I had started riding. I did not dare tell her it had been on a travellers' horse, but I must have touched a nerve in her of some sorts. She offered to pay for riding lessons for me in central London on the weekends I was away from Barnardo's.

Of course, I had to look the part. We went off to Moss Bros for some new riding gear, which we kept at her house. The lessons were like heaven. One would think that a young black girl, wearing the finest of riding gear and taking lessons at one of London's elite riding schools, would bring sideways glances and consternation, but I cannot for the life of me remember anyone ever saying anything to me or Janet about it. I just remember the riding. Janet stayed and watched. I do have to acknowledge her for giving me that gift, for horses have saved my life on more than one occasion.

It was around this time that I left Miss Toad's cottage and was placed in one in which the matron liked me. This is reflected in my annual reports. I also began to attend the local Jewish Girls' School, which was a big change. It was going to that school and leaving the Barnardo's atmosphere which allowed me to find pieces of myself, and discover what I was like on the inside.

I was allowed to walk to and from the school. I made friends, and felt liked. Sometimes I would stop by my friends' houses for cups of tea and maybe some food. I can remember families who seemed perfect – polite, caring and nice. Thanks to my life with Janet and her family, I fitted right in and liked it.

My class work was still not good, thanks to my dyslexia, but I excelled at sports and was very popular. I was even voted Class Captain. My personality was allowed to shine. I was given space and the respect to be a young girl. Barnardo's could not allow any of its children to experience individuality or individual attention, but at the Jewish Girls' School I felt like a normal girl. Only my brown lace-up standard Barnardo's-issue shoes gave me away.

I loved the two-mile walk to and from the school. I loved the freedom I was allowed. Outside the walls of Barnardos', laughing and joking came easily to me. And even though my schoolwork was not great, I was lucky enough to have some very good teachers. The woman who taught religion at my new school was lovely and respected me as an individual; consequently, I did very well in her class. She was able to see me not just as a troubled coloured girl but also as someone with an opinion. I will never forget her.

Around this time I began an after-school job at the local stables, so I was working with horses and riding all the time. It was bliss. The paperwork has reports from my employers and status on my working conditions and performance. My records, unfortunately, do not include reports from my new school. I wish they did. I would like to see, in black in white, how the individual attention and respect I remember so distinctly affected my performance. Here again, I am left with only memories.

It was when I began to work at the stables that I finally began to come to terms with the colour of my skin. The atmosphere there brought home the truth about my skin and living with it in the UK. I was blatantly left out of most after work activities. The social aspects of working there just weren't available to me. Many times people just talked over me, or through me. Of course the people I worked directly with had to acknowledge my presence, but the clientele ostracised me completely.

It is strange that life was so normal at times and at others so abnormal.

Growing up in care is one thing, but growing up in care with family visits and a normal school experience is another.

Now my father was getting older and his health was not good. The weekends I saw him began to be about me looking after him, rather than him looking after me. The Barnardo's paperwork reports his health to be failing at the time, but I did not realise it at the time. I just thought he was tired and getting older. I was happy to look after him.

The time I spent with Janet then started to change. I still went off on summer holidays to her cottage and had my own room, but our relationship began to change. She stopped my riding lessons. She took an interest in a boy from London, an orphan. He started coming with us to the country and staying over at her house. I used to always play with Janet's son, Edward, but now there was another child around. To be honest, I was jealous.

I can see now that she no longer saw me as a child she could use as a charity case to make herself feel better – she needed a replacement. I was starting to talk back and ask difficult questions. Despite what she had done she was the only true mother figure I had, and her shutting me out was hard to take.

Of course at the time I had no idea why she did this. I do now, but then it was just another wound in my psyche. I should have seen the signs, but I was young and happy, attending a new school, working with horses, seeing my dad. So what if Janet was not so nice to me? I was still out of Barnardo's on weekdays and at weekends. I thought it couldn't change.

Most Barnardo's children stayed in school until they were 16 and learning a trade or skill, when they would be found an apprenticeship or work placement. But my father's health was now deteriorating fast, so when I was 15 I left the home early to care for him.

I was thrilled - no more school and no more Barnardo's! The paperwork reveals that they wanted me to find a permanent job, but Dad's health quickly became the main issue. There were no stables in Camden Town, so I stopped working with horses. Instead, I got a job at a local pet store. I was still working with animals, and I was close to Dad.

After I moved back in with him I began to notice how ill he had become. He wasn't working at all now, so all my wages went towards helping him and paying for our food. I did manage to save up enough to buy a television for him to watch, and I was very proud of that.

Most people would think that a 15-year-old girl should not have to live in a dingy one-room basement flat with a sick old man to care for after working all day. But I loved being with him and being able to care for him. I did not see it as anything but normal, especially since I was free of the strict rules and schedule of Barnardo's. I was living with my dad, and I was the happiest I had ever been. I had freedom, I was self-reliant and I had someone to love and to love me back.

At weekends, when he could manage it, we would resume the old pattern to our lives, taking walks and watching telly together. I even brought home a puppy, which I called Snowy, and spent hours walking him in Regents Park. There were ups and downs to Dad's health, but sometimes he could meet me for lunch or we could go places on my days off. Other times he was home, ill and in bed.

I do vaguely remember seeing Janet during this time. I might have gone with her a few times to her cottage at weekends. But my memories are filled with my father and spending all the time I could with him. I still did not realise how ill he was. He had breathing problems and his hands were shaking. The paperwork documents his health as 'unstable'. I was allowed to leave only to care for him and find a job to support him.

The letters reveal that it was the social worker assigned to me who found the job at the pet store so I could be with my dad. I was still being watched and monitored, but I was oblivious. Instead I felt fulfilled and complete. I loved being at the pet store and remember it as a very good job. Everyone was very nice to me and seemed to like me, and I liked them. Independence was something I badly needed. I was earning my own wages and paying my own way.

My father was hospitalised very soon after I went to live with him, though the memory of that only returned to me after reading over my Barnardo's paperwork. I stayed at Janet's house with my new puppy Snowy. We went away for the weekend and I had to return to her house for work on Monday.

Reading this made me see how much a part of my life she still was. The other thing I realised was that she was the Barnardo's contact and appointed fosterer for me. It makes sense that she was still a part of my life at that time. The paperwork also shows that the social worker was in direct contact with Janet and her husband. It is eerie, to this day, to think that I was always being watched and checked on by the authorities during a time when I felt such freedom and independence from Barnardo's.

One day in December 1964 I came home for lunch to find Dad wasn't there. He had been having bad spells, getting forgetful and finding it hard to breathe, so I was very worried. I rushed out and ran through the streets of Camden, shouting and desperately looking for him. The panic was overwhelming.

It seemed that someone had found him wandering the streets in a daze and for some reason, he had been taken to a psychiatric hospital. The hospital was far away from Camden and with my work schedule as it was, my visits were only at weekends. It was an odd time for me, and my memories of it are very grey. All I can remember is working hard, caring for the flat and the puppy and getting to see Dad as much as I could.

After Dad went to hospital I lived in the flat on my own and then moved in with a friend. I was under pressure from Barnardo's about living without a guardian, so I moved in with an Irish family who had pets and did not mind my Snowy being with me. I went back to the flat to clean and check on things. I remember wanting to keep it nice for my father to return to as soon as he was better.

The copies of the reports from this time show concern on the part of Barnardo's for my well being without a proper guardian. It is still hard to understand why they could not just leave me be. I was working and I paid the rent on the flat myself. I fed and clothed myself. I saw my father in the hospital. I was independent and free of all the bureaucracy of the institution that was Barnardo's. Yet despite this sense of independence, they were watching me. They still had dominion over my life.

I will never forget the day they came for me. There was a knock at the door, and I opened it to find a social worker and someone else. They explained that under 21s were not allowed to live on their own, so I was to be taken back to Barnardo's immediately.

'But I am OK!' I said. 'I have a job, my Snowy, look at the flat, it's clean, it's paid for! Look around, I am fine! Leave me alone!'

They would not listen. That day is burned on my mind forever. I was forced to return to Barnardo's and live with other children again.

I went mental. After many fits of rage and screaming, I was put into a room on my own, with my dog outside. This whole part of my life has had a huge effect on me. I was back being controlled again. It felt like a prison, yet I had committed no crime. For a time, everything went black.

So much else was detailed and documented in my paperwork, yet my memory of the social worker removing me from my home is simply not there. It remains the deepest scar from this period of my life. How strange that I have letters referring to social workers watching me at work, but nothing about that horrific removal from my home. It is such a huge part of my life, yet there is nothing to support their decision, nothing to tell me why they had to do it. Once again, I get the feeling that if it wasn't documented, it didn't happen.

For a time I lived in a cottage in my own room back in Barnardo's. I was miserable. The only saving grace I had was my new job. I was dedicated to it. I was hired as a stable hand at the Riding Centre for the Disabled and I loved it. The wages were low, but I was with horses and could help people. It was all my heart desired.

Barnardo's was many miles from the hospital where my father was being cared for, and I was working so many hours that my visits were few. His condition worsened and he turned into a true invalid. Yet seeing him made me happy, and if I could just hold his hand I felt everything was ok. He was completely immobile and could not speak, but he could squeeze my hand.

The last time I saw him he had been moved closer to the matron's desk. When I could not find his bed and asked where he was, I felt an ache in my stomach I had never felt before. I walked right past him without recognising him. They had put him closer to the matron's desk because he was dying. I know that now, but back then I had no idea how truly serious his condition was. No one told me.

I find it shocking now, after having worked in care all of these years, that no one thought to counsel me about it all. Not one of the social workers from my paperwork, or an auntie, or anyone at Barnardo's, warned me that my father was going to die. Even Janet was silent. Yet I was 15 years old, I had cared for him and he was the only family I had.

Reading through the copies, I searched desperately for a reference to a conversation I had perhaps forgotten, a social worker who had explained his condition or braced me for the sadness. There was nothing. I thought he would get better and that we would go back to our flat and get on with our lives. I thought it was just an illness.

I have blocked out so much of my life, but the day I found my home had been taken away I will remember forever. After one of my weekend visits to him, I called at the flat to check on things. My key did not fit the lock. I knocked and a stranger answered. He said someone from the local council had cleared out all our things. Everything had been taken by council workers to make space for someone new. All my family photos, all my things, all my father's personal effects, were gone. They had taken our radio, our beautiful long cabinet - everything. The built-in cupboard was cleared out and all our clothes and personal things had gone. It was like a robbery.

No one from Barnardo's had told me this was to happen, nor was I asked to be present at the removal. Why not? Did we owe money? Why didn't they arrange for my things to be collected? This would never happen today. Our whole life was disposed of, thrown away. My father and I had been erased. We had disappeared.

I had nowhere else to go but back to Barnardo's. Going back to work in the stables was my only salvation. The horses were my home now. The smells and the animals were my solace.

Then one day, my boss came to tell me there had been a phone call from the hospital. My father was dead.

A phone call! Not one of the so-called carers, or Janet, or an auntie could come and tell me and hold my hand. Just a phone message.

I went to the hospital. I was supposed to collect my father's effects. All he owned was a ring and a watch, and that was all I had from him.

The funeral was in Hebrew. I vaguely remember being accompanied by a male social worker. However, my clearest memory was of another man, a man claiming to be my father's brother. His words to me came from nowhere and scarred me so deeply.

'Can you prove my brother adopted you?' he said. 'No of course you can't. I want nothing to do with the likes of you. And that ring you have, it's my mother's. I want it back!'

The social worker said nothing to help me. I was not in any frame of mind to say anything. Even though now I know Barnardo's had the proof of my adoption records, they once again did nothing to help me when I really and truly needed it.

I handed over the ring and never heard from my father's brother again. My paperwork from Barnardo's makes reference to the fact that my adopted uncle was in contact; he was not. Any overture he made to Barnardo's on my behalf was just that, an overture. The only memory I have of him was the day I met him at the funeral.

After my father's death I was in a state of shock. I had lost my past and my future, along with the only person who truly loved me.

There is nothing in my paperwork from this time to indicate that anyone took any interest in my well-being. No one from Barnardo's helped me through my grief, and neither did Janet. Only John Davis, the man who owned the stables, extended any kind of hand to me. He was a hard man, yet he saw my grief. As a special treat, he took me into the depths of East London to look at a horse for the stables. No one else showed me any kindness or concern. Janet Darlington did not show up at the funeral, and she offered me no words or cards of condolence. I have no idea why. I tried to contact her, but I heard nothing back.

I went back to work the next day. I just got on with it. If you were to ask me now which was more traumatic, the loss of our flat and our possessions or the death of my father, I would have to say that each was as terrible as the other. I will never forget either loss, for they were the only two links I had to who I was. Nobody else knew me or cared about me. My past had been buried; it no longer existed.

Most adopted children will experience, at some point after entering adulthood, a burning desire to know their genetic past. With the death of my father, I had lost all ties to my birth mother and her story. This realisation did not hit me until later on in my adult life, but it still casts a shadow over my thoughts today.

My father must have been the most progressive man of his generation. Literally - he adopted a black baby girl. He tried as hard as he could to raise me. He never stopped loving me. He was a pioneer of his generation. Janet Darlington could try to assuage her middle-class guilt by caring for under-privileged kids, but my father was the real thing. I know now that it is his love and devotion to me that have saved me. As a person who has worked as a carer most of her life, I have heard every story known to man. Horrible stories, stories like mine. But then I was on the other side of the desk. I am someone who cared, who could find enough love not to hurt myself or others. That strength comes from him.

CHAPTER FIVE

Switzerland and Italy

After Dad died, I was allowed to move into the stables and live in one of the bungalows with another girl called Helen. We did shift work, and because I lived there I did all the shifts for anyone who did not show up. I was constantly working from early mornings till late at night. I loved it, and it meant I was away from Barnardo's.

I had one day off a week from the stables and no longer had to check in at Barnardo's, but my papers reveal that they were checking on me. They were in contact with John Davis and he was reporting back to them. Funnily enough, in my folder there are applications made on my behalf by Davis applying for sponsorship to pay for my qualifications for riding. I never did get a sponsorship.

Then John Davis left for America, so I left too. Without the personal connection I had with him and his wife and the meagre salary I was paid, the job was not one I could have kept. Nobody was going to sponsor me to get my riding qualifications so that I could teach properly, so a future in horses was just a fantasy. After all, I was black and the riding world of Britain is a very white one.

After the stables job I took a cleaning job in a home for the disabled and lived with a couple called Mr and Mrs Hale. I was also in correspondence with one of the assistants from Barnardo's, who was Swiss. Margaret and I had formed a friendship when she was at Barnardo's and we continued it through letters after she moved back home. She was kind to me and I trusted her. She was one of the few.

It was one of Margaret's letters that planted the seed of my leaving the UK. I wanted to be rid of England. I needed a fresh start. My father's death had left me completely alone in the world with no true friends and no social life. There was no excuse not to try my luck out in the world.

In 1968 I was still considered a minor because I was under 21. Barnardo's would have to arrange and facilitate my leaving the UK for work in Europe. Margaret found a position for me as a nanny with a Swiss-German family. I did not realise at the time all the paperwork that would be necessary for me to go - passports, visas, train tickets, etc, but somehow I managed to acquire all the things I would need to leave the UK. I had no idea where Switzerland was; I thought all countries had sea around them.

The UK social services had an office in Basel where I was to go and they were informed of my new job, residence and employers. They were watching me even over there.

Funnily enough, I still have the suitcase Barnardo's gave all of us on leaving and going out into the world to work. It was packed with everything I owned (which was not much), along with Noname, my bear. I travelled by train to Paddington, and at some point I must have gone on a boat to cross the sea. I can't remember the crossing or the sea. I do know that for the whole 16 hours of the journey I chatted to people around me. I was very excited about this journey. I was off!

This part of my life set the precedent for many more moves in my future. Each time I feel a time of my life has passed, I search for every opportunity to get as far away as possible, reinventing myself in the process.

Basel in the early morning was a sight to behold. The train station was an alien planet to me. The harsh guttural sounds of Swiss German and the smell of coffee were all around me.

I was picked up by Herr Schrarer, my new employer. He was a fat scowling man, and I took an instant dislike to him. We drove to his house in the suburbs. His wife was very tall and slim and she was much more pleasant. I had to share a room with their eldest daughter, Anne Marie. I had been promised my own room, but at that point I was so tired that I fell straight into bed. The next thing I remember I was being awoken and told to start to work. It seemed I had only slept a few hours, as indeed I had.

The job was OK at first. The job placement description was for a nanny to four children and nothing more, but I was now told that I was also responsible for all the washing and for cleaning the entire house.

I had cleaned before this job and I have cleaned since, but never have I encountered so many rules and regulations about cleaning as there were in the Schrarer's household. One of the silliest was having to clean and rinse all the dishes before putting them in the dishwasher. Once a week I had to scrub the entire house clean; I even had to take all the water out of the toilet bowls and wash them completely.

There was a big front room with a large carpet, and Frau Schrarer asked me to comb all the tassels straight every day. The families' underwear had to be folded three times and put away neatly every morning. I rose early and made breakfast for the children, and every night I fell into bed exhausted. I had one day off a month and a half day off a week – that's all. I worked the hardest I have ever worked in my life. It was nothing short of slavery. Nothing I had been promised before I left was delivered. But I was 18 and naive, and I would never have thought of going to the social services office and report the family for violating my work contract. I think Herr Scharer knew that.

I met no one. I had no time! Except that occasionally, on my days off when I wasn't sleeping, I went to Margaret's house. She had her own family to care for and was pretty busy, but the few times I went to her house for dinner were lovely. I couldn't say anything to her either, for fear she would think I was ungrateful. I endured the work.

My employment with the Schrarer family did not last long. After a few months it was the Easter holidays, and I went with the family to the mountains. It was the first time I saw those mountains, and they made me feel very small. The air was exquisite. The children and I had fun together outside playing and since we were not in their home, I did not have to clean as much.

Herr Schrarer was not a father who spent much time with his family. He was constantly working. This holiday time forced him closer to them, and it proved to be a problem.

Anne-Marie was his oldest. She was a lovely girl, but she was entering into her teenage years and beginning to question authority. It was hard to include her in our games, and I think sometimes she felt a bit left out of everything. I tried to include her and find different things for us to do. She and I shared a room, so we were pretty close. I cared for her, and she for me.

Her father had no time or patience for any of his children, but especially for her. His authoritarian ways did not work with teenage rebellion. He would not recognise anyone talking back to him at all. The tension between father and daughter grew until one day, he went into a rage and hit Anne Marie in the face. I ran over to her to check on her and he screamed at me to leave her alone. He sad she deserved to be punished for talking back.

Something inside me snapped. I reacted to Herr Schrarer's violence with violence of my own. I beat him and beat him.

Of course, I left immediately. I wish I had not reacted in that way, but, somewhere deep down inside I hoped Anne-Marie was safe from her father's hand.

A tribunal of Swiss authorities reviewed my work visa, and somehow I was given permission to stay and carry on working. I think Margaret might have helped me. Luckily I found a job at a Jewish home for the elderly, working in the kitchens. It was a wonderful job. The kitchen staff were all from different parts of Europe and we lived in a dormitory on site. Everyone had a story they did not want to tell, so no-one asked. Even so, there was an underlying bond between us; we were all lost and looking for something. And that suited me just fine.

The kitchens in the home were kept kosher. Two fridges, one for dairy and one for meat; two sets of bowls, utensils, knives and pots. It was fascinating to learn all the reasons for the rituals, and being around older Jewish people made me feel so much closer to my dad. I heard Hebrew spoken and listened to their stories. I knew my father had changed his name after the war to escape bullying and prejudice in the UK, but hearing these people's stories of survival and loss made me realise the true severity of what it meant to be Jewish.

There were lots of staff, not just in the kitchen; there were carers and cleaners and assistants. We all became friends and spent our free time together. At last I felt I belonged to a group. My boss, the chef, was a hard taskmaster, but he was fair. He had a deep belly laugh and told some pretty lewd jokes.

It was here, in this happy place filled with raucous laughter and hard work, that I met my first boyfriend. He was Italian, with dark curly hair and smiling eyes. On our days off we just walked, from park to cafe and back to the park again. We danced at parties and drank dark black coffee. It was innocent and lovely.

I was so happy that I never wanted it to end, but Paul was needed back in Italy. He wanted me to go with him and I wanted more adventure. Now I had a taste for a different life - for different foods and smells and the sound of laughter.

Paul told me there was a job going as a nanny, and I went to the UK social workers' office and requested a move. Yes, they were still watching and monitoring. But this time I gave them the minimal amount of information. I wanted to be lost in my own life and not have to report in anymore. I escaped.

There is a pulse in Milan. The women are gorgeous and the smells divine. Paul had arranged for both of us to get jobs in the city, me as a live-in nanny and he as a waiter.

Nannying did not last long. I am not one to sit back and watch children be mistreated, so I left and went to work in a nice little Italian hotel run by a good Catholic family. My Italian was passable then, as was my Swiss German. I worked the front desk. On our weekends off we went to the mountains above Lake Como, where Paul's family lived. They took me in as one of their own. The views were magnificent, and I can still see the mirror-like lake and taste the crisp air on my tongue.

My job in the hotel came with a room, which I shared with another girl. She worked nights and I worked days, so we rarely saw one another. After a while, it came to light that she was a 'working girl'. The family were mortified, and forced her out immediately. I was guilty by association, so I was fired and told to leave as well.

I went to live with Paul and his family, and he said he loved me and asked me to marry him. I tried to convince myself that I loved him too, but I didn't really. He was a kind and good man, but my feelings were not that serious.

As a promise, he gave me a small heart necklace, which I still have. It's funny, there are many decisions I wish I could make again in my life, but marrying him is not one of them. It was not meant to be.

I soon had to go back to England and fix my work visas for Europe. My next job took me back to Switzerland and to one of the happiest times of my life. I went to work for one of the first Conscientious Objectors of Switzerland, Herr Meyer. He had founded a community up in the mountains, building holiday chalets for people from poor countries. It was one of those working vegetarian communities. There were lots of people from other countries, and I loved it. We physically laboured all day and spent lovely evenings sitting round campfires singing songs. On our days off, we would rush down to the little village and buy all the sweets and meat we could get our hands on. I learned to mix cement and build with stone, and how to build fires and start them outside without matches.

Herr Meyer was such a kind, good man. He told us why he hated war and illustrated his opinions with horrifying stories. He would protest when he could, and he wanted us to protest too. Thanks to Herr Meyer, every time there is a demonstration against war, anywhere, I stop, watch and listen, and if I can I walk with them.

The work placement visa for the Swiss Alps lasted six months. In the end, I had to return to Britain. On the way back, I went via Paris with one of the girls I met on the work programme, and stayed there for a month. I know students who take gap years or go off travelling do this all the time now, but back in the 1960s it was rare, especially for a working-class black girl who was still a ward of the state.

Ah, Paris! There is something so magical about that city. I did not feel out of place or too foreign. I wanted to go back and see it all again.

When I returned to Britain at the age of about 21, I was on my own. Barnardo's no longer needed to watch over me or send social workers to check up on me. They did, however, suggest that I move into the YMCA in Romford. Being someone who usually did as she was told, that is where I went. It was a new building which had one floor for the girls and the rest for men. At the local café was a posting for work in the local factory, and I took it. Now Barnardo's was out of my life for good.

This was certainly not the Alps, and the factory job was loathsome. I spent my days putting nails into boxes with a strange machine. I longed for the physical work and the feeling in my muscles after a day of building – standing in the same place all day is the worst thing someone can do – but I needed the work and the routine. Adjusting to life again in Britain was hard, but I was confident and knew I was capable of doing any task asked of me. I had travelled in Europe and lived in Switzerland and Italy. There was no social worker to watch over me. I felt young and free.

Living at the YMCA I came into contact with all sorts of people, mostly men. For the first time I got to know a black man. Obame was African and took a real interest in me. Up to that point in my life, everyone I had close contact with had been white. He seemed strange and different, and I must admit he made me feel a little displaced and even more self-conscious.

All we ever did was chat in the dining room at the YMCA. I was fascinated by his story and wanted to know what it felt like to live in his black skin. He in turn wanted to know what it was like to live in a white world. It was the first time in my life that I realised how unusual my life had been so far.

I was extremely sheltered, and sex was still a complete unknown. Even though I had had an Italian boyfriend, I knew nothing of the ways of men and women or of the sexual world. Not one person had ever thought to sit down and explain it all to me. Of course, I knew about animals and could somehow connect that act with babies, but the actuality of if all was truly foreign.

Paul and I had kissed and held hands, but his family never let us share a room when I went to visit. Not one of the rooms I had had allowed for male visitors. In Barnardo's it was never discussed, and there was no sexual abuse - ever. At least it was a safe place for us children from the evil in the world, even if there was a lack of love and compassion.

My relationship with my African friend was just that to me, a friendship with my first black friend. The other men I met living at the YMCA were just people, ones I said hello to, had a laugh with, or a moan. The men at work were the same. Some even reminded me of my dad. I was so naive.

Two months passed. My room was lovely; I had a peach-coloured bedspread which I had got for nothing from a charity shop. There was a kettle to make tea. I had a table with two mismatched chairs. People would float in and out of each other's rooms.

Men were not allowed on our landing after 10 at night, so I was surprised one night when someone banged loudly at my door demanding to come in. It was Joe from Tahiti. I had only ever seen him in passing in the dining room. Obame never spoke to him and always looked away when Joe walked into a room. And, even though I was so innocent of the ways of the world, I trusted Obame.

I was quiet and pretended not to be in, but Joe heard me and started yelling loudly. I was so scared I would get into trouble and get kicked out that I opened the door.

This is another part of my life I wish I could go back to as my adult self. I want to hold my own hand and pull it back from that door handle. When someone means to harm you, you quickly realise what is about to happen, and Joe was there to harm me. He was drunk, and although I had no idea what that truly meant, I knew he was acting like an animal. My animal side took over and I fought for my life. I was young and strong, but physically I could not match him. He was over six feet tall and at least 17 stone, while I was barely eight stone and five feet four. I fought at first, but then I began to realise that if I kept fighting he would too, and he could have killed me. I stopped kicking and pushing and biting and fell limp and lifeless. The cloud of realisation turned into a black cloud, and darkness came. I knew he was hurting me, I knew he was raping me, but I was separate, removed. It's the only way to survive something like that.

Joe disappeared from my room and I lay still and breathed slowly. After a while, when it was quiet on my landing and completely dark, I limped down to the community shower. The water turned a strange pinky-red colour as I showered. It stung as it hit my burning skin. I could not wash it all off.

I looked for Joe afterwards, but he had disappeared from the Y. I was too scared to report the incident. What if they kicked me out for having a man in my room after 10 pm? I could not hide my bruises, so I told people I had fallen downstairs.

I went back to work and acted as if nothing had happened, but then after a month or so had passed I began to feel ill. Since I had no idea about sex and what happens if you have it, I had no idea the state I was in.

I lost weight, I vomited. I was exhausted. I was pregnant, and had no idea. It was my friend the night porter who told me what was wrong with me. He knew Joe had disappeared. I am sure, looking back, the porter knew what had happened to me. He saw me every evening when I came home from work. I would always stop and chat and have a laugh with him, but after Joe's visit, I became remote and cold and lived behind a wall of blackness.

The porter knew when I rushed for the toilet in the main hall after my walk home from work. When he finally asked me what was wrong, I told him my symptoms.

'Should I see a doctor?' I asked.

'Yes, my girl, as soon you can. I bet you're pregnant.'

I didn't understand how it had happened, so he explained it all to me. 21 years old, and I was learning about the birds and the bees from the night porter! But he was a kind man and could obviously see how naive I was. He wrote down the name of a local doctor who could help me. Even though I had been raped, I felt ashamed and wanted to punish myself.

Abortion was my only option. It was legal, but only just. It still carried an enormous social stigma, so it had to be kept very secret. The doctor made an appointment for me, and as with almost everything in my life so far, I did as I was told.

The hospital was cold and sterile and the ward was full of other women who had either had children or were in the throes of labour. The doctor who performed the abortion was horrible - unkind and cruel. He told me that getting pregnant was my fault, and he is the reason I have never had another male doctor since.

While I was recovering in the hospital afterwards, even the nurse treated me as if I was a prostitute and told me this procedure would probably be my usual method of birth control. How little they knew! I wanted to scream at them that I had been attacked, that I had fought for my life, that I had only been allowed to live because I had played dead. How could they treat me that way? It is shocking to hear this story today. Our society has come a long way in 40 years, but, if you ask me, not far enough.

I went back to life in the YMCA. Much as I wanted to keep this all to myself, I couldn't keep it all in; it was eating me alive. I wanted revenge.

Most of my friendships at this time of my life were with men – strange but true. One man, an Indian called Patel who worked with me, was to be trusted. He had a large family of sisters and aunties and spoke of the females in his life with a great reverence. I often went to their flat for family meals and felt a part of something.

I told Patel about the attack, with the idea in the back of my mind that maybe he could help me to find Joe. We looked everywhere we could think of. He went to other boarding houses in and around the working class areas of London. We did not have much to go on, though the search helped me a little. But Joe had disappeared, and I was left with more scars.

Rape is as different an experience for different people as life itself. I handled it the only way I could – I packed it up and put it on a shelf high up in the loft of my mind. Then I left it there. I did not trust men, but I still wanted to be friends with them.

Obviously I became more cautious, but I got on with it. Today there would have been groups I could seek out, or a support worker to give me strength and the ability to cope. But back then Britain was a different place, and I was lost in its uncaring world. I buried the rape as deep as I could, but it was still there.

Again, I needed to move. A fresh start, a clean place. Something new. I saw an advertisement for a bedsit in Ilford, so I took it. My new landlady was hard, but honest and fair. I found a job with a pharmaceutical company, caring for the animals it was using for testing. The job was sad at times, caring for animals that were being abused so badly by the tests performed on them. It was a true eye opener for me. I knew there was cruelty in the world, but here it was blatant.

I worked an odd schedule, sometimes including weekends, and my free time was spent wandering. I made a few friends from the neighbourhood and work, but I kept myself to myself. I still felt ashamed about what had happened to me and thought people might be able somehow to see into my mind. Crazy, I know, but it was a defence mechanism.

I started to retrace the walks I had once taken with my father. I remember that winter being particularly cold and dark. I tried to keep myself focused on the animals and the few friends I had, but I wasn't that strong.

In the bedsit, which was in a large house divided into several rooms, there was only one shared shower. It cost a shilling, but it didn't give you a shilling's worth of hot water. My room was L-shaped with a small window and horrible yellow curtains that neither provided warmth nor provided shade from the sun. There was a good lock on the door, which I used, but I bought an extra chain and installed it myself.

Most of the other occupants of the house were men. Obviously, to get to the shower I had to wear a dressing gown. I was so desperate to leave the Y that I did not think about the effect this would have on me. I was vulnerable. The shower room door did have a lock, but it wasn't very strong. Scenarios started to play up in my mind which I could not black out. I began to suffer from what I now know to have been panic attacks. I could not leave my bed at night. A weight would descend on my chest and hold me prisoner to my fears. The days, which had previously been bearable, were turning dark, and my fear invaded them too.

I stopped caring about cleaning; dirty dishes piled up and unwashed clothes were everywhere. I can remember throwing plates at the walls. I could not stop myself.

Then I began to go out walking alone at night, hoping for something to happen to me so it would just end. I called them my suicide walks. Subconsciously, I knew I was losing it. I had nowhere to turn for help. All those years having Barnardo's to watch over me had left me strangely more vulnerable than anyone could be. No one cared any more. I was truly on my own, in the blackness.

The blackness, the panic attacks and the suicidal thoughts have been a part of my life ever since the day I was signed in at Barnardo's. I can't explain the coping skills I used. I consider myself a brilliant actress. If I am forced to stop acting and the coping walls I have built around me come down, the frustrations and sadness find a way to get through. I shut down. I don't talk, I don't challenge. I don't lash out. I go quiet. Without expression, without revealing any feelings even to myself, I begin to refer to myself in the third person.

When someone asks me to talk about 'it', I do not get it off my chest. I can't. I do not feel better writing these words. I never feel good about anything when this fog descends down on me. I am in a rage. Every traumatic event in my life has been completely and totally out of my control, as trauma often dictates. I had no family, no real friends, nobody to help me and love me and hug me and let we weep on their shoulder. No outlet for my grief. It's still there inside me, like another dimension, another me.

The life I have had so far has been nothing but trauma and heartache. Now I am looking back, and I am angry. I will not have another family, another love, my own house. I am at the end of my time and I cannot get it back. None of what has happened to me has been through any fault of my own. Life happened to me. I have had good times, but they do not override the horrible things that are still with me on so many levels.

Many people have said 'You should see someone' or 'Maybe therapy can help you'. I get so angry when I hear this. How can people think you can make a lifetime of trauma and disillusionment could go away just by talking to someone? I do know myself. I don't hurt others, I don't take drugs or drink; I did not beat my children. I actually care and want to help other people. I have to wonder where that fine line comes from. But when the black comes, I just have to shut down.

One night, aimlessly walking and daring danger to come for me, I met a man. A black man. He was lost and asked for directions. I realised from his accent that he was American. He was well-spoken, kind and felt from the beginning that he needed to save me. And maybe he did, just a little.

His name was Terry. We began meeting for walks around London. He was there for business and wanted someone to spend some time with. I never felt any danger from him, only kindness. He was the first person to show me any of that in a long time. He never made me feel uncomfortable or tried to touch me, he was a friend. And he came along when I needed one the most.

We went to dances and parties. I usually asked one of my friends from work to come along with us. Helen and I were invited to a dance at a hotel and as a treat he got us a room, just Helen and me. It was the first time either of us had been in such a grand hotel. You could leave your shoes out overnight and there they were the next morning polished, ready to go. My shoes – me, the girl who used to have to polish 42 shoes on a Sunday at Barnardo's, having her own shoes shined!

Terry was a good man and he was falling in love with me. He did not know about my dark side, and being with him kept it at bay. I could forget about the darkness inside me, force it deeper down.

I asked him many questions about his family and what their lives were like. I needed to hear his stories, as I felt a huge connection to him. I so wanted him to be a long-lost cousin, a member of my family. I was happy spending time with him, but I could not love him; it just felt so familiar with him. Also, my silly young self believed in true love back then. I was waiting for that feeling that my friends mooned over and the dramas portrayed. Much as I liked Terry, there were no butterflies in my stomach. Now, I would not think twice.

He wanted to take me back to America with him, buy me a house and make me happy. Can you imagine what could have happened? Me in America; maybe I could have found my birth father; maybe I would have been happy. I know I broke his heart when I said no. He left quite suddenly, and I was all alone again.

I did however have my first full relationship while I was living in Ilford. For a long time after I was raped I had found it hard to let any man near me, but there was one exception – Matt. He was a very nice man who loved me to pieces and treated me like a princess. He did not pressure me in any way, so I trusted him. But I did not enjoy the sex with him; I felt no attraction. It was not the fact that I had been raped, more simply that he was not a good lover.

CHAPTER SIX

Country life

Janet Darlington was still on the fringes of my life. She was the only mother figure I had known, and cold as she was to me, I sought her out. Terry was gone, and I felt broken. Maybe I wanted solace, though that was something I knew she couldn't give. Maybe I wanted her to hold me and comfort me and tell me it would all be OK.

We all seek a mother's love when we need it, even if that mother is cruel and emotionally abusive. It's a phenomenon I saw working in care. Young adults, or for that matter children, taken from abusive homes always want to go back to their abuser-parent. They still love them, and even if trust is broken, the child will always want to be with the parent again. It's their family. It was the same for me.

Of course, Janet offered no love. I seriously doubt she was capable of that. But she offered the next best thing, money. She was always trying to improve my station. She wanted me to go to secretarial college, and she gave me some money and said I could buy a car or a horse.

I chose the horse. Cilla was black and white, not too big and part thoroughbred. I had to stable her miles from where I lived. I took my saddle and bridle back and forth with me, walking half a mile to and from the bus stop.

It was worth it. Horses always have saved me, and Cilla was my anchor. I saw her three times a week, at least. Riding her saved me from the blackness, and caring for her, knowing she needed me to feed her, kept me getting out of bed each day. I saw Janet only once after she gave me the money, when I was living in Suffolk later.

I had a little motor scooter which gave me freedom, and I rode around Essex and London, putting many miles behind me. I left my bedsit and moved to another, and another, and another. I kept changing jobs too.

I was often refused accommodation or jobs because of the colour of my skin. I did not make new friends easily and only really kept in contact with the friends I had made through the stables. I was poor, but I survived, with Cilla and my little scooter.

After black periods of my life, a sort of greyness comes. I feel as if I am just going through the motions of living, moving here and there. Just floating along.

There have been times when a glimpse of a man in a trilby hat like my father's would cause me to run after a shadow. In my mind he was still walking the streets of London. I heard his voice calling me. I would follow the smell of pipe tobacco to its source, only, of course, to be disappointed. His ghost was everywhere. It was years before I stopped seeing him, hearing his voice, smelling his smell.

After moving from bedsit to bedsit for a while, I finally moved into a two-bedroom flat with a friend, Karen, whom I met through working at some stables in Enfield. We got on very well. In the summers I had a job with Battersea Children's Zoo, a mobile zoo that travelled around to visit kids in different places. It was brilliant. Working with animals and children is a dream for me. Although I was floating through my life, this was a good period.

There was a woman called Joanne who worked at the zoo, and she fell in love with me. She wouldn't leave me alone. This was my first encounter with homosexuality. As with ordinary sex, I had no idea there were people in the world who had sex with their own gender. I was completely naive to how that world worked.

It happened when I went to meet everyone from the children's zoo one night for a drink. Karen and I walked in and failed to notice we were in a gay bar. We should have realised when we saw that the woman at the door was dressed like a man. All kinds of people were done up in what I thought was fancy dress and dancing to some really good music, so we had to join in.

Joanne started to stare at me intently. She tried to dance with me and pressed herself up to me. I truly had no idea what she was trying to do. Then, out of nowhere, a man in a silver catsuit came to my rescue. He pushed Joanne out of the way, started dancing with me and asked if I was gay. When I said no, he laughed and told me I was in a gay club. Karen and I tried to leave quickly, but Joanne would not stop pressuring me. She kept staring at me and tried to go out of her way to touch me. I did not return any of her advances and tried to avoid her, but she was obsessed with me and could not leave me alone.

Finally she got so angry that I was ignoring her that she attacked me. I stood my ground, but I was flabbergasted that a woman could have such strong emotions for another female. I learned quickly after that how to avoid gay bars and not to be friendly to any woman who gave me long intense stares.

I worked for various stables around Essex and for the zoo in the summer. It was not much money and very hard work, and I knew I needed fundamental change. I have always buried myself in a new life to escape an old one; it is a pattern I recognise and accept.

Since childhood I had always wanted to be a nurse, so I searched out hospital jobs and found work as an auxiliary nurse. The hospital was in Enfield, and I lived on the premises. It was a unique place, exclusively for the elderly. One of the wards held a group of elderly people labelled 'mad' or 'mentally unstable'. In reality, they were a sign of their times. This was the late 1960s and some of these women had been in this 'hospital' for 30-40 years. The common factor was that they had all had babies out of wedlock. For this, they were seen as 'loose women'. Their babies had been taken away and they had been put in the 'hospital' for treatment.

I cared for them and memorised their stories. I was so close to being one of them myself. The stigma of having a baby out of wedlock had changed somewhat, but not much. They were not mad of course, they were sad. I identified with them a hundred per cent.

I was new at the hospital, so all the cleaning jobs fell to me. When I was asked to wash a dead body on my own I did not question it, though I found out later that this was not the hospital's policy. Seeing the body caused me so much anguish that I began to weep uncontrollably. The head matron overheard me and consoled me as best she could, but the damage was done. I can still see that grey corpse and feel its waxy skin.

The sister who left me on my own received a reprimand from the matron, and this left me with an enemy. There is nothing worse that working with someone who hates you. She did everything she could to make sure I was miserable, and since I lived in the hospital as well, I had no true escape.

The strange thing about it all was that she was black too. I thought that because we shared the same skin colour she would have been a friend. I have since learned that some black women can be quite aggressive to other women of colour. It's only when you stand up to them and show them you are not afraid of them that they will back down.

One day I had had enough of this woman. I hit her and locked her in a cupboard. After that, she became my friend and invited me to her house for dinner! Very strange.

I was at the hospital for at least a year, working all the time. My horse Cilla was so far away that it was impossible to get the time to make the journey to see her. I ended up selling both her and my scooter. I worked shifts and my schedule very rarely coincided with that of my friend.

I withdrew into my work. I loved the patients and listened to the life stories. I wanted to hear about them, and they needed to tell someone. They needed to be heard to prove that they existed. I knew that feeling, so I listened.

I had a friend who lived in Suffolk and on my rare weekends off, I visited her and we went riding together. One weekend she mentioned a cottage just up the road which was for rent. I walked up to see it and fell in love with it immediately. Janet had spoiled me with her weekends in the country. London was not free enough. I needed to get out.

As soon as I could I left London and moved to the cottage my friend had found. It was small - two bedrooms upstairs and a small front room downstairs with a scullery/kitchen. There was an outdoor toilet, but no bath, and I had to wash in the kitchen sink, but it was my own place!

I found there were not many jobs to be had in the countryside. I cleaned when I could and worked at various local stables. I was happy to be free of the city and its oppressiveness. There is a certain smell in the countryside, a cleanness found nowhere else.

I got a job cleaning the local pub outside opening hours. The landlady was a horsewoman like me, and we became very good friends. Though I was not a drinker, I met many of the local patrons and soon had developed a bit of a social life. I was the only black person for miles around, and it was in that village that I really began to experience the full brunt of racial prejudice.

I discovered through my cleaning work that the local hotel was being refurbished and they were throwing out their carpet. It looked perfectly fine to me - it was typical hotel carpet, much like a pub's, very brightly coloured. As I dragged it down the road, I laughed out loud as the locals nearly ran off the road staring at me. I carpeted my whole cottage with it, even the outside loo.

Life in the country was good to me. I was working all the time, cleaning houses and working with horses. I liked being busy. I liked the feeling of using my body and being physical; I always have. I settled into a nice routine.

The pub was the centre of the village, and it was there that I met James. He was quite posh. His father was the ambassador to some island in the Caribbean. He and his family seemed very comfortable around me and my dark skin, not at all like the many of the other people of the village.

I went to their dinner parties and ended up talking to diplomats from all over the world. James was a typical middle-class child who had nothing to rebel against but felt he had to rebel anyway. He and his friends thought rebellion was all about drugs, and James wanted so badly to be thought of as a hippy. His parties were notorious and filled with drink and drugs. I went to them, but never really felt at ease with the drinking or the drugs. I was much more at home in the stables or riding in the countryside.

It wasn't James who ended up winning my heart - he eventually left and went to the Caribbean with his father - but one of his friends. I spent more time at the pub with my friend Alice, and it was there that I starting bumping into Charles. Alice mentioned that he had been staring at me for ages, even when I was with James. He intrigued me.

The first time I remember being properly introduced to him, he was helping out a tree surgeon. He popped his head down to say hello when I passed by with Alice. He was blond, tanned and fit. He started coming around to my cottage fixing things and hanging out and it was not long before we were dating.

Charles and I were very attracted to one another and our sex life was very fulfilling to me, at least at first. Most relationships are good in the beginning, and ours was no exception. I was happy with Charles. He made me laugh, a lot. And, since my experience with life was limited, I failed to see the obvious signs that being with Charles, however much fun it was, was doomed. He drank - all the time. He never stopped. I thought it was just good fun, at first.

After we had been dating for six months or so Charles asked me to marry him, and I said yes. I loved him and wanted love in my life. I no longer wanted to be on my own, struggling against everything; I wanted to have someone in my life who was mine and I was theirs.

His family was nice, though they were different from anything I had ever known. I realised this when I met his room-mate, a very nice older woman called Mary I will never forget the time Charles and I were driving back from their cottage to mine (this was before he had moved in with me) and I said 'I like Mary, she's very nice. How do you know her?'

'She's my mother' he replied. I was speechless.

Charles and Mary talked about art and music together as if they were the same age. She was a brilliant pianist. His whole family was into the arts, and there was always someone visiting from London. Music was played, drinks were poured and the conversations were always so witty. No one called each other Dad or Mum or Granddad or Auntie - it was all first names.

I liked Mary straight away and she liked me. She was a very beautiful woman. She listened to me and asked me questions no one else had ever bothered to ask. She was a captivating person, but not someone you would ever guess had children.

Their relationship was odd at best, and that should have been my first clue. What do they say – make sure the boy is nice to his mother before you marry him? No one ever gave me any advice, and I had no family to warn me or give me an example. I didn't know how relationships were supposed to work. I was so naïve.

Strangely, Janet Darlington's cottage was only about 10 miles away, though I never knew that at the time. I had been very young when we used to go there. When I realised how close she and Tom were, I wanted to visit. I went to see her for Mother's Day, took a card and made some fairy cakes for her. She barely acknowledged me, except to insinuate that I had come to her because I wanted something. She called me ungrateful.

It broke my heart. I lost my cool and shouted at her. Her attitude made Tom really angry. He could plainly see that I had come just to see her, to talk to her and to share with her, and she just seemed, once again, to throw me away with a disappointed look on her face.

I still wanted Janet to come to our wedding; there was no one else for my side, no family for me and all my friends were Charles' friends too. She refused to come, though Tom came. I was forever grateful to him for it. I never saw Janet Darlington again.

The wedding was at the local register office. I can't remember why, but I broke with tradition by going there with Charles instead of getting ready at my friend's and going to the ceremony from there. I took care with my appearance, as all brides do; I had on a beautiful dress. I do remember him telling me that I looked nice. But the one job he was supposed to take care of, to order and pick up a bouquet of flowers for me at the florists, he didn't do. We were late for our own wedding because he had to stop at a local shop and grab some cheap wrapped flowers. How could he have forgotten?

The rest of the drive was a nightmare. My internal voice was screaming, 'Don't do this! He couldn't even buy you flowers for your wedding day!'

I wouldn't listen to the voice. I wanted to marry Charles because I wanted desperately to have my own child. I had wanted a baby for a long time, and he wanted to give me one. There was no way I was having a child on my own, without a husband. In the back of my mind were those poor old women at the hospital, and I knew I could not end up like them. So I ignored his oversight and pushed that little voice down deep inside me.

To make matters worse, when we arrived at the register office, a funeral procession was just leaving. But my desire for a family was strong. I ignored the omen and walked right in behind them.

We said our vows and signed the register, then went to Alice's pub. I had a few drinks (Charles had a lot more than a few) and that was that. We were married. There was nothing magical about it. And the little slip of paper, now our bond, could not stop the drink from flowing. It proved not to be the cure but an excuse for him to drink even more.

I didn't understand addiction then as I do now. I wish I had, because I would have run away. As it always does, the addiction became the dominant force in our life together. Charles drank more, while I worked harder. The arguments were intense. But I wanted to make it work, I wanted a baby. I wanted so hard for the family dream I had to come true. I turned the other cheek again and again.

Finally I became pregnant with our son, Leon. Charles was over the moon, but of course he celebrated by going to the pub.

I was sick throughout the pregnancy. Charles was not very sympathetic, and had given me a lot of emotional and verbal abuse. He was a clever man, and his words were cleverly mean. His actions were manipulative and selfish. But the first time he tried to attack me, I wasn't expecting it.

He was drunk, so there was nothing different about this time from any of the others. I managed to pry myself out of his grip and escape to Janet's pub, and I stayed there for days. Charles came to plead that he still loved me, that he needed me, he wanted me. He begged forgiveness. I have to believe that he was sorry. But, as I know now, it was the exact reaction all abusive men show towards their partners after they abuse them.

·

I had nowhere else to go. I didn't want to be pregnant and on my own. I had no family to turn to, no one to help me. It was a different time then, and there were no government agencies to help women like me. I could not run away and hide in a halfway house. I felt as if I was in a box with no opening.

I went home. It was the only thing I could do.

The violence and the abuse escalated, as they always do. It's never a one-off with abusive drunks. His drinking was steadily getting worse and worse. I always left the door open and food out for him before I went to bed, but one night I forgot. I woke to the sound of him screaming and breaking plates. He came looking for me and punched me in the stomach. A rage to protect my unborn baby took over; the kettle was on the work surface and I grabbed it and hit him as hard as I could. Charles fell to the floor, completely knocked out.

I stepped over him, walked out of the door and went to the pub. Janet took me in and got me into see the local doctor the next day. My baby and I were both fine. I should have stayed away, but I was trapped in a cycle of abuse that becomes a way of life. It's never normal; it just is. I went back to Charles, but this incident caused the baby to arrive six weeks early.

I went straight into full-on labour, with no intervals between contractions. The hospital was 15 miles away from our cottage and I was screaming the whole way. The trip would have been ok if Charles had not stopped to look at some badgers. It was so typical of him - there I was in agony, and he wanted to watch badgers.

Leon's birth took two days. Today I would have had a c-section. The pain was excruciating and I will never forget it. When he finally came out he was not breathing and completely blue, but somehow I managed to sit up and plead for them to let me hold my baby. They revived him, he took his first breath and they put him in my arms. Horrible as delivering him was, when he was in my arms it was worth everything.

After his birth I had stitches internally and externally. After I had spent few days in hospital recovering, we went back home. I can't remember much except having to walk in the bitter cold to the neighbours' house to bath. I'm sure I had post-natal depression. There was no midwife to come to your home and check on you and the baby, no health visitor to see if I was well. It was just me and Leon, alone. I tried as best as I could, but I knew nothing about babies.

It was during this time that Charles's mother became ill. She was still teaching the piano in London, but at the weekends she now needed someone to look after her, so we moved in with her at her cottage in Mount Pleasant. Charles found a job with a roofer in London, so he was gone as well.

The weeks were long. There were no shops within walking distance and I had no car. Most days I was lonely and at my wits' end. When Mary came home at weekends it was a relief to have her company. She was wonderful with Leon and a very adoring grandmother, and it gave me a little time for myself.

Nothing changed with Charles. He went on drinking and staying out until early morning. My attention was focused on Leon and keeping him safe. I did everything I could to appease him, so much so that I got pregnant again. However bad things were with Charles, I still wanted to have another child. It was important for my son to have a sibling.

When I was about three months pregnant I suffered a miscarriage. Luckily Mary's twin sister was visiting and she took me straight to the hospital in Colchester. I was sad, very sad. I still am. Having a miscarriage is a horrible experience for a woman.

We couldn't stay in that place, it just was too remote. But one of Charles' drinking partners had a solution. He was a rich man with a massive country estate that needed looking after, and there was an annexe for our little family.

CHAPTER SEVEN

Cutting loose

Jack Bruce was nobody to me, but he was a big deal to a lot of people because he was part of the rock band Cream. They were in their heyday and Jack had so much money it was silly.

His house was massive. I was the housekeeper and Charles worked as gardener/handyman. I kept the house running smoothly. It was hard working for Jack - his life was erratic and his marriage was on the rocks. But it was a beautiful house and I loved having Leon there. The garden was beautiful and Charles did an excellent job keeping it that way.

But it was chaotic, and I could not be in a chaotic marriage and witness another one at the same time. We left after only six months and got work on another estate as caretakers.

Charles' drinking continued unabated. There were times when he tried to dry out, but to be honest the detoxing was almost as bad as the drinking. He would constantly nag me and seemed to be fixated on himself and his problems. His mother's health declined quite rapidly, and he was trying so hard not to drink during the same time. I know now that he was suffering, but his narcissism was very hard to take. And it was very hard to be living in close proximity to other families when our own was so hard to deal with.

When Mary died she left us a small inheritance, which enabled us to leave caretaking all together and buy ourselves a lovely little home in Glemsford.

Charles had lots of ideas for the house, and that was the problem. He would start a project and never finish it. The worst was his attempt at exposing the beams in the loft, which was our bedroom. To do this he somehow had to remove a floating ceiling which protected us from the damp, the cold and snow. He took it off but he never finished the job, leaving our bed exposed to the elements.

After Mary's death, he went back to the bottle and his drinking was the dominant force in our lives. He was more aggressive this time, but I learned to cope with his moods. My main focus was to keep Leon away from it all. Unfortunately I could not always protect my son and myself. If I locked the doors, he would just kick them in, so I kept them open.

I did everything I could not to let his shouting in the night wake up our son. I would get up as soon as I heard him stumbling in and make him something to eat. I listened to his rantings and ravings just to appease him and keep him as quiet as I could.

It wasn't long before I became very ill. I was so tired all the time and it felt as if I was always walking on eggshells. No matter what I tried, Charles would inevitably smash up the place, throwing things around and breaking anything he could find. Then he would want to talk, and he would talk endlessly. A lot of it was rubbish, psychological mumbo-jumbo about himself and his problem. He never wanted a response or an opinion. I was scared to say anything to him when he was in this condition.

He would then fall asleep. There was a time when I would clean up after him and his rants, but I stopped doing that in the end. I had to stand up to him somehow. Sheltering Leon from it all was my main goal in life.

Several times I looked up the stairs to see Leon shouting 'leave my mummy alone!' He absorbed it all. My gut instinct was to protect my boy, and I couldn't even do that. His little face was a horrible thing to see.

This sent me into a deep darkness. There was a time when I had to check myself into a psychiatric hospital. I can't remember what I did with Leon or how I ended up there, but it was a dark time for me. I was a victim in it all and there were times when I had to call the authorities for help. But Charles was such a good liar, and in those days the police almost always sided with the man when they were called out on a 'domestic'. Not to mention the fact that I was black - I had no chance. Once I even tried to drive to Wales to escape him, but he reported the car stolen and I had to come back.

I also started to see to see that it was not just alcohol; it was the person he was, too. It was his arrogance. When he did try to stop, he would just want to talk and talk about himself and his addiction, all the time. Then he would go back to the drink, and the cycle would start all over again.

Although living with him was making me weaker and weaker physically, there were a few times when I turned on him. I am not proud of my violence towards him, but I was like an animal fighting for its life. I was at heart a fighter, yet my spirit was broken. I could not leave - I had nowhere to go. No family, no close friends.

By the time Amy was born, I knew I no longer loved Charles. I wanted my daughter, I wanted her so much, and Leon was ecstatic over having a sister. With Amy he was so loving and caring. There was never any jealousy or rivalry between them as siblings, only love. And that's what I say when people do ask me about my marriage, that I have my two beautiful children. That is my blessing from it all.

In his own way, Charles loved his children. His aggressive and vile behaviour was reserved for the women in his life. Leon saw it, though Charles never turned on his own son.

He had always been verbally abusive to his mother while she was alive. There was even a time when his sister came to visit and he started to raise his hand to her as well. I'm sure he would have hit her had I not stepped in.

His behaviour now seemed normal to me. Every action in my life was influenced by Charles's anger and its outcome. I tried to anticipate his every mood swing, his every tirade, his every movement. But as every person who has been a victim of abuse knows, it is impossible to keep the peace for very long.

Charles was not some thug from the back streets; he was from a middle-class family. One of his ancestors had been an Archbishop of Canterbury. Everyone in his family was educated and seemed to be well to do. Charles's parents were bohemians who decided to live very different lives.

Charles's sister was about 15 years older than he was and consequently had a very different upbringing. She was sent away to school and sometimes came home at weekends and holidays. Charles was more like her child that he was his own mother's. His parents were artistic and free-living. His father had been an alcoholic too; he had died when his son was only 15.

Charles had been brought up by two people who shunned conventional parenting methods and let him live with no boundaries or structure. He was a 'free range child' who seemed to have just raised himself. He had no discipline; he was allowed to do and say anything he wanted. And when his parents moved to the country, Charles was sent to the local school. Other families would have sent Charles to a private school, where his potential would have been realised. He was way too posh for the local comprehensive. To top it all off, he was extremely intelligent - smarter in fact than most of the teachers. Yet instead of going off to college and finding a career that suited his level of intelligence, he stayed in Suffolk trimming trees and repairing roofs.

Our marriage continued on its destructive path for a while after Amy was born. But every relationship has its turning points, and I will never forget the moment I had the first of mine. It happened the winter after she was born, when we had snow coming through our roof. We had an Aga, so we had to have the fire lit every morning to heat the house and the water. Of course, Charles was usually out cold at that time, so I had to split the logs and carry them in and light the fire.

That freezing cold morning I had my first realisation that I really wanted my husband gone from my life and the lives of my children. Charles had come home early in the morning, and I had stayed up to cook for him so my children would not be woken. I had slept for about three hours. I went outside to get some wood, then came in and lit the Aga. I was kneeling over the opening in the front and holding a metal poker. Charles chose that moment to wake up and start tormenting me. Something inside me just flipped, and indescribable anger and rage took over.

I came to my senses hearing Charles shouting my name over and over again. The red-hot poker I had just been using to stoke the fire was now at his throat. I was on top of him like some sort of animal. I know that if he had not shouted me back to reality I would have killed him, and that scared me to death.

The final turning point came about six months later, on my birthday, July 24th. It was pouring down with rain and Charles left that morning with no explanation. I called a friend who came over, and she asked after Charles. I had to explain to her that my own husband had abandoned me on my birthday.

We took the kids to her house and she got a sitter to watch them for the night. Bless her, she took me for a meal and tried to pretend it was all OK, but we both knew it wasn't.

When we arrived at my cottage, Charles showed up, drunk. My friend told him off and then left, leaving him in a very agitated state. He turned his anger on me, as he always did. He was enraged, worse than I had ever seen him. I was so frightened that I wet myself. The realisation of the state of fear I had been in for so long was enough to propel me to action.

The next morning Charles was out cold as usual on the sofa. I crept out of the house, careful not to wake him. I dropped Leon at his pre-school, took Amy to a friend's house, and then I went straight to a solicitor. I had never in my whole life been to a solicitor, but there was something inside me that said 'you have to survive'. I could not ignore it.

I walked in and said I needed to make an appointment, but the man saw something in my eyes and invited me to come in there and then. In a shaky voice, but with determination, I told this stranger I wanted to divorce my husband.

Charles could not keep a solicitor; he would not show up, or if he did, he was drunk. It was the easiest divorce I have known. The court knew instinctively that the children should be with me, and I was awarded the house so that I could bring them up. The funny or rather, strange, thing was that Charles was ordered to pay exactly £1 to me for each child per year. I still chuckle at that. A pound a year to feed and clothe and educate our children! I chuckle even more thinking that of course he never paid a penny of it.

You might think that it would be over, now that he was out of our lives, but it wasn't - far from it. Charles wanted 'us' back and could not face the fact that his children were no longer his to be with. I have no idea where he went or how he survived financially. Strange men knocked on my door at all hours demanding money that Charles owed to them. Charles himself would come and bang on the door harassing us. It was a nightmare. Once again, my world went very dark, and this time I had two children to care for with no support at all.

I think I was completely broken at this stage of my life. When you live your life armed and ready for an attack, and then the threat has gone, the breath and space that comes after is very hard to deal with. All the negative energy and emotion of my past came crashing down in the aftermath of my marriage.

For the time being, I knew I could not care for my own children. I made the hardest decision I have ever made and put them, temporarily, into care. I just could not give them the attention and love they needed when I felt so broken. I needed the time and the space to make some good decisions about our future. It broke my heart.

The best thing I did during this time was move away. I loved my little cottage, but I needed to cleanse myself of it all. I packed our things and moved to another town, where I could breathe and think. I was in a different space, and that was good.

After about three weeks I took my children back and felt stronger. But Charles found us, and the harassment worsened. He claimed that he wanted to see his children, but every time we made arrangements for him to see them, he failed to show up. Then days later he would bang on the door trying to kick it in, demanding to see us. Drunk, always drunk.

I had to look for work that fitted in with the children's school hours. All I could do was clean other people's houses and businesses. I walked dogs and did any odd job I could find. Somehow, I made it work.

Living in that little town was better, in the sense that I had more opportunities for work and shopping was much easier. But most importantly, my colour and my children's, particularly Leon's, who has a darker skin was not such a major issue. It was an issue – just not as serious as it was before.

Charles's sister Mary had married and moved to Bristol. After our divorce she kept in touch, as Leon and Amy were her niece and nephew. I think she always knew in her heart how hard it was to be with Charles, so when she suggested that we move to Bristol so she could offer some sort of support, I was happy to do so. I wanted to be as far away from Charles as possible. So I sold our little cottage in Sutbury, packed everything up and moved to Windmill Hill in south Bristol.

Leon and Amy went to school just down the road from us, and we made friends and became a part of the neighbourhood. While the children were in school, I worked as a cleaner. I soon got a job at a home for the elderly, where I got to know a man called Dave. He helped me to buy a second-hand car so I would have some transport.

Dave and I became very close as friends and I began to rely on him for many things. It was nice to have a man in my life who was honest and dependable and whom I could trust. We had some very good times together.

And then – he committed suicide. It came as a huge shock to me. Dave was like the brother I had never had, and I went through another of my dark spells after his death. I tried not to let the sense of abandonment and isolation beat me. I knew his suicide was not a personal affront to me; it was his only way of dealing with his demons. It still took some time for me to find a better place emotionally. Watching my children grow and become little people was the antidote I needed.

All in all, Windmill Hill was a happy time for me and for my children. We had a nice house, the school was good and close to us and I had a good job. Every weekend we were out and about visiting friends and going on adventures. We take holidays camping in France. I was still a single mum, surviving, never finding it easy, but happy.

Leon and Amy were sociable children and had loads of friends, but they were still two children who had been the victims of abuse and violence. Leon, my beautiful little boy, witnessed more than his little sister. Because of that, he experienced many problems growing up. He was a handful, and tested me time and time again.

Charles did not help. Almost invariably, Charles he failed to show for his scheduled pick-up time. His blatant absence from Leon's life made things worse. He never once came to Bristol to see his children. When he did make it to one of our arranged meetings at one of the services on the M4, he was so late that the children were asleep in the car. The time he could have spent with them was over. That does something to kids, and Leon and Amy were no exception. They suffered a deep sense of abandonment which I could not fix. I suppose that is why, now, I make myself available to them all day and all night. I never say, 'No, I cannot come.'

Otherwise life in Bristol was good to us. The reason for our move was to be closer to Charles's sister, but that never really happened. We fell into our own life and routine in a completely different part of town.

Yet I found Bristol a slow city. I wanted a more vibrant black community for me and for my children. I wanted my children to know what it was like to be in the heart of a community that accepted them. For that, we needed to go to London. It is where I am from and where I needed to return.

So I sold my house in Windmill Hill and bought a home in East London. It was an experience that shaped us all. My kids went to school where they were not different; they were normal. In London they had friends of colour and dual-heritage. I too was in my own skin again. It was what I thought we needed, though looking back now, I wish I had never left Bristol.

Leon and Amy settled in eventually, but Leon was a challenge from the start. East London was not a good place for a young lad growing up and trying to prove himself. I did my best to keep some sort of order in our lives, but Leon did his own thing, and most of the time it involved some very bad choices. There were many, many nights when I did not know where my son was, who he was with or what he was doing. When he was at home he was sullen, moody, even violent at times. He was so angry.

Finally, in order to protect my daughter and myself, I took away his key to our house so he had to knock on the door like everyone else. It's a hard decision to ask your own child to leave your home, but I had to do it for my own sanity and for Amy.

When Leon left home our lives became more normal, but I worried about him constantly. Leon was on his own path and Amy was on hers, working in the Hackney Empire Theatre, making friends and loving living in London. And I was back in London, where my brown skin was not an anomaly.

By now I was in my mid forties and was feeling a definite pull to realign my life and find some peace and tranquillity. I had heard about a place that sounded like the perfect solution, a nunnery in Kent. The waiting list was about a year, even for just a long weekend retreat, but after a long wait, I got a room.

We were allowed to speak only before 7 am and after 7 pm. The facilities were basic and no outside communication was allowed. It was completely silent. It was summertime and the grounds were lovely. I remember reading in the sun, and sometimes crying on a bench. No one came to ask me what was wrong; no one interrupted my feelings. Silence was the key.

Being alone with my own thoughts made me realise just how away from myself I had become and how much I needed to find out who I really was. I realised that I had been someone's daughter, then a ward of the state, defined by an institution, and then I was just floating along looking for something. I had been a wife and I had been a mother, but I couldn't find 'me'. The understanding came like a wave on a beach – I wanted to find out who I really was.

Going back into London on the train was a shock to my system. The noise was like crashing cymbals all around me. I needed something more than what I had – something more basic and quiet. Something with solitude, where I could look inside and find out who I really was.

In London, I did several jobs cleaning and caring. I worked hard, saving and scrimping. I saved every penny I could, knowing that I wanted out of the mayhem and the noise.

CHAPTER EIGHT

Jamaica

I moved to London to be close to other black people. We all fitted in and I liked that, but now I had the knowledge that I needed something more, just for me, and I needed the silence to find it. I also wanted to know what it was to be completely submerged in a culture of black people. And to be honest, I was tired of working. Amy and Leon had become their own people and I no longer had to provide for them. It was time for me to have an adventure of my own.

If someone in my life had offered me a place to stay somewhere in Africa, I would have taken it in a second. Instead, Jamaica was the first option that came and I jumped at the chance.

I saved my money, rented out my house and bought two tickets to Kingston. Amy came with me - she wanted to have an adventure too. She was always one to land on her feet. Leon stayed in London, living his own life.

When I boarded the Air Jamaica flight my heart lifted and I felt a deep sense of attachment forming. Everyone was black, even the pilot. During the flight there was a fashion show with Jamaican clothes. It was the best flight of my life. I couldn't wait to shed my British clothes and change into the island's attire.

When I stepped off that plane, I was home. The humidity was intense and I thought the heat was from the engines of the plane, but it was just the hot climate. It felt like warm butter on my skin, and I loved it.

All I could see was an ocean of black faces. And I was one of them; it was a whole culture just for me, like me, the same. I had never experienced a true sense of belonging anywhere, until then. Most black people in the UK have families in Jamaica to go home to, but for me there was a connection irrespective of blood or family – I felt I was home.

My initial plan was to stay with a friend of a friend, an older gentleman called Tim Henry who lived in an area away from Kingston on the east coast, called St Thomas. It was not touristy at all. The Jamaican culture was pure. I have never been happier. Mr Henry, or Uncle Tim as we called him, wanted someone to drive him about and do some light shopping, and it was an easy life. He did not ask much of me and I had tons of free time to explore and get to know the island.

I stayed with him for one magical year, and it flew by. No one can know exactly what it is like until they do it – just to leave your old life and step into a steamy tropical paradise. Life is slow, hot and full of surprises. You never know who you are going to meet or who is going to come into your life.

Amy stayed with me at Mr Henry's house too. He had a definite opinion about young women and how they should behave. Amy, being a modern young woman, did not fit into his archaic ideals. He was constantly harping on her about her male friends and going out without a proper escort. He could not understand friendships between girls and boys. Amy explored on her own and made lots of friends. She learned the local language and could fit in, but Mr Henry made her life unbearable all the time she was in his house, and after five months she left.

I stayed. I had found my quiet, my peace. I adapted very well to the island's way of life.

A few months after Amy left, I became very ill with an unidentified infection. I was prescribed some tablets to take, and they almost killed me. Within days, I developed headaches and a severe rash. I could not stomach any food. My arms and legs swelled to double their size. The pain was agonising and for two or three days I couldn't walk. I could hardly leave my room, and I barely managed to get in a taxi. Taxis in Jamaica are always shared. The people next to me were just brushing my legs, but to me it felt like they were burning me with a lighter. It was agony.

I managed to make it to the doctor's, but had to wait with all the others patients. The doctor finally came out to call another patient in, but took one look at me and rushed me through. She injected me with something and then paid for a taxi to take me directly back to Uncle Tim's. She was so concerned about me that she came to visit me that same evening, injected me again and explained to me that I had sulphur poisoning from the tablets. Luckily for me, she had been trained in the USA and was a caring doctor who went an extra step for me. In fact she saved my life.

.It took me weeks to recover. Jamaican culture dictates that you just have to get on with life, so that is what I did. I did realise that the last place you want to be in hospital is in Jamaica, at the mercy of the Jamaican healthcare system.

At the end of the year I returned to the UK, determined to go back there to live. I was now on a mission. My desire to be back in my adopted home was a pull I had never felt before. In London I did three jobs, saving every penny. Then, about six months later, I sold my house. Hindsight is 20/20, but I probably shouldn't have done that. I'm not going to dwell on 'what ifs' - I did what I felt I had to do at the time. Jamaica was going to be my home now.

This time Leon wanted to come, and I agreed, as I wanted him with me. Amy was joining us later. We flew into Kingston, and finally I felt I was home.

At first we went to live with Mr Henry again. He was completely different with Leon - he was a man, and Uncle Tim treated him as such. Taking Leon to Jamaica saved him. While he was in London his environment was dangerous, and getting him out of it was the best thing we could have done. When he did get into trouble in Jamaica (it was inevitable for him at that point in his life), the local police put the fear of God into him. He was so scared that he never got out of line again. There are rules in Jamaica; there are no second chances. It is a very harsh world for anyone who wants to try and challenge it. Leon rebelled and tried to challenge the rules, but he learned his lesson, and for that I am grateful.

I wanted my own place, a home for my kids to come and go, so we stayed with Mr Henry just long enough for me to find a place we could call home. The house I found was about five miles away, in a little parish called Pomfret. It was a small bungalow in about half an acre of land, just off the main road to Kingston. , and it was ours.

Pomfret is a part of the island where there is an enormous salt lake with crocodiles. There are a few secluded beaches, used only by the locals. It is a very low-key place. A normal day consisted of waking up at 6.30 am, making tea, washing clothes and maybe going down to the market for some shopping. In the afternoon we went to the beach and slept (you had to sleep in the heat of the day, it was so hot). We spent evenings chatting with the neighbours and strolling around the village.

I was not working now, and life took on a new pace for me. I was just living and getting by. The days went so quickly. It was easy to make friends because we had stayed with Uncle Tim before and we had a tie to the community. We had a social life and explored the island, visiting different friends and their relatives.

Kingston was an exciting city to visit. Everywhere you went were black faces. When you remove the concept of prejudice from your life and live in a world where you are just like everyone else, you have utopia. Obviously there was a divide between rich and poor - there always is in third world countries - but no one was singled out for their skin colour. No one followed me in the shops, no one crossed to the other side of the road.

Life on a Caribbean Island is lovely - sunshine, blue seas, fresh fruit - though we did get hurricanes. Pomfret is down at sea level, so getting to higher ground was important whenever a storm blew through. The rainy season gave us huge storms, sometimes hurricane strength, and the seas would rise and the winds would blow so hard. Most of the time when the weather took a turn for the worse we would leave our little bungalow and go back up to Uncle Tim's, because his house was higher up the hill and more protected.

About six months into our stay a hurricane came, so we took shelter at Uncle Tim's all day and all night. When we got back to our house we found a tree had fallen on to it and it was flooded. Once the weather eased, our neighbours came out and we all started to help each other. Our furniture was put out into the hot sun to dry along with our clothes and other things. It took quite a few of us to get the tree off the house.

We waited a while for everything to dry and then we swept out the house. The landlord came a few days later and repaired the damage to the roof. There were no dramas, and better still, no insurance adjusters to deal with. That's the thing about island life - you just get on with it. No one fusses, they just help each other out. I miss that.

The kids fitted in well and really took to life in Pomfret. They made lots of friends and were constantly going off to explore different areas. Amy really learned the local language, Patua, and made a point of getting to know all the locals. It was wonderful for her to have freedom. She gained even more confidence within herself. I never worried about Amy. Even though she is very light skinned, she could speak the language and hold her ground with anyone. She and Leon began to do some modelling in Kingston for an agency. They were making their own lives on the island and I was happy that they were happy.

But life has a way of catching up with you, and I was no exception. One day I was on the road back to Pomfret when someone overtook me on the inside while I was turning, and crashed into me. He drove away quickly, and those who witnessed the crash started after him. I was badly injured and had severe concussion.

The last thing I wanted was to be stuck in a Jamaican hospital, but now I had no choice. I had to stay for three days, in a big ward with men and women all lying side by side. There was no bedding or food, nothing - your family were supposed to provide everything. When someone died - and they were dying all around me - the body was carted off right in front of the rest of the patients. It was horrible. It wasn't until the day after the accident that they got around to x-raying my head.

I walked out of the ward as soon as I could. My van was collected by a friend who was a mechanic, and he repaired it for me. I was happy to see that my loose cash and all my music were still inside, untouched.

That experience was horrible, yet the support and love I felt from our friends gave me a wonderful feeling.

Then the woman who owned our bungalow decided to sell it. We looked for other properties to rent in Pomfret, but there were none. I did not consider going to another part of the island - everyone I knew was there and we were part of the community. Jamaica is a place that operates on people knowing people - strangers are not welcome.

Around the area were some empty houses that would have been perfect - some were just down the hill from me. According to local folklore, they were inhabited by the 'ghosts of the family'. As on many islands of the Caribbean, the old ways are the way. Although the island is very Christian, witchcraft, or Obi, is also taken very seriously and many of the locals believe in both. Ancestral ghosts are an important part of the island magic. Once you have lived there it all starts to make more sense.

I tried to convey my respect for their beliefs and said I did not mind living with ghosts, but the owners of the empty properties still said no. There was nothing else to rent in the area, and I started to feel lost.

They call the interior of Jamaica the 'bush' – it is wild countryside, with few main roads and not many signs. Everyone knows everyone, and strangers are even less welcome than they are on the coast. I had met a few people from the bush, and had been told of a house which was available for rent.

I went to have a look, and decided to take it. Although my connections were only through introductions, this seemed to be enough. I still had to work hard at making friends and being accepted as someone who could live there.

At first I did not have a car, so I walked or took buses. Finding work proved difficult. The problem with most third-world countries is that there are no opportunities. I had a three-year permit which allowed me to work, but it could not help me find work. I quickly realised that the opportunities just were not there, and my savings were going fast.

I had to find a way into the system – and as I have learned in my life, hard work is best. I bought a van and began to do taxi runs and sell coconuts in Coronation Market in Kingston. Those who know Coronation Market will know that for an Englishwoman to go there alone is a little crazy. But I didn't see danger – I saw opportunity.

I paid for a small space and set up in the market about twice a week. The market was a whole new world, and one I loved. I felt a part of something and was slowly accepted.

The taxi was competitive and to be honest, a bit dangerous. In order not to upset the local taxi-driving mafia, I focused on the school run. They needed rides to school and I was there to help them. It was a guaranteed income and seemed safer. The kids would pack themselves inside like sardines.

I did manage to make a living, albeit a small one. My life was simple and living in the bush turned out to be something I could connect with, but it was a hard way of life.

My children were doing well, and they would come and go from our little open-air house in the bush. Leon fell in love with a young girl from the other side of the island. He wanted to be closer to her and her family, so he moved in with one of her aunts. When I went to visit him, he was happy and very settled. As a mother that is all you really want for your children.

Amy was with me off and on. She had friends she would go and stay with, but I think she found living in the bush a bit harsh. Life was raw and the people were on the edge of everything. People would fight over petty jealousies. Life was just not as precious as it is in other places, and Amy witnessed some very vicious attacks.

I was running out of money, and helping her with living expenses was draining my savings. She was ready to go back to the UK, so that's what she did. After she left, I was sad and I missed my daughter, but I knew she was in a better place in the UK, working and staying with friends.

I was still driving my 'taxi' but did not have the proper paperwork to be a taxi driver, and soon had to give up my van. It didn't matter, because my needs were really simple. I soon adapted to the bush way of life and was living simply without spending too much money.

An ordinary day revolved around bathing and washing in some springs near my home. My walk there every morning kept me very fit, and the location was pristine. Walking through the countryside and bathing in natural springs became a normal part of my life. It is surreal to me now to think that. There was such beauty and simplicity to my life.

The bush is not a place for a woman by herself. People talk, and men start to come around. I did not want the attention - I wanted to be left alone. I had my dogs to guard me and keep me company.

I did have some male friends, one of whom was a local man called Steve. He could fix most things and he would come to help me with things around the house. It was nice to have someone strong to help move and carry and clear the brush. My house was simple, but it still needed to be maintained. Steve was a quiet, somewhat moody man. He never made any moves on me, and I appreciated his presence in my life.

The Jamaicans thought that because I was English I must be rich and gullible. I had to stand my ground. More importantly, I had to live as they lived in order to gain their respect and eventually, their friendship. But I spoke differently, I knew more about the world; I was more educated. I tried as much as I could to live like a Jamaican so that I wouldn't stand out so much. I bathed and washed my clothes in the river. I walked everywhere I could. I waited with them for taxis and buses. I ate Jamaican food. I spoke the local dialect and never put on airs with the way I spoke to people.

Jamaicans are a very superstitious and religious people; the way you live and what you say is important. The secret to living in the bush as an outsider is to have the right balance between aggression and being timid.

My days now were much simpler than they had been in the bungalow. All my time revolved around water. My day consisted of waking with the sun, walking to fill the water buckets and having breakfast, followed by a bit of washing and feeding the animals. By midday it was too hot to do anything but nap. Once it cooled off you could bring in your washing, walk to the river for more water, have a chat with your friends, and then dinner-time comes.

You have to bathe twice a day because of the heat. Jamaicans are fastidious about bathing, and I was surprised at the cleanliness of the people and even more surprised at how devout they are. I have never been around such religious people. Every other building is a church, and everyone goes to church. It is a big part of daily life in the bush. Although I never went myself, I respected those who did.

I lived in the bush for two years. It was a simple but lovely way of life. Anyone in the UK would have considered me below any poverty line they could imagine, but to the Jamaicans in the bush, I was rich. I had my own house which I had to share with no one, while most of my neighbours had to live with their extended families and in-laws. I had privacy and space, and to them that was luxury.

Leon was in and out, but he basically lived on the other side of the island with his girl's family, while Amy was back in London. Steve soon became more than a friend. It was a good relationship. He offered security and company when I wanted it. However, by this time I had been there for about two and a half years and money was very tight. There were no more taxi runs and no more selling coconuts in Kingston. I was not eating properly, so I was getting quite thin. Jamaica was also becoming politically unstable and divisions within society were deepening.

Jamaica is a poor country with no infrastructure. It is corrupt and dangerous. At the end of my stay the country experienced one of its worst periods of modern times, the petrol riots. The price of petrol controlled everything on the island, because if you couldn't get to Kingston to sell your wares, you couldn't eat. The tax on petrol had become outrageous and after one rise the people reacted violently. Roads were blocked and almost all supplies were cut off. Transport became virtually impossible. Jamaica was on the brink of a very violent situation.

I was on a trip to Kingston with Steve when things started to become deadly. Luckily Leon was on the other side of the island, where people lived a simpler life and were more spread out. He was safe with his new family. I was worried about myself now. When it was time for a general election, Kingston disintegrated into something close to civil war, with gunfights, road blocks and fires.

Because of the roadblocks Steve and I couldn't get home, and we were forced to take refuge in a township called Port Moore, on the edge of Kingston. We were trapped in the middle of a war zone. I could come and go on a limited basis by claiming to be an American missionary, which the police and soldiers believed. The road blocks prevented any food coming in, and when I did manage to get to the market in Kingston, it was very scary. I had to keep my eyes focused straight ahead. I wore no colours that might have somehow indicated any sympathy to one side or another, and never made eye contact with the armed soldiers in Tiffany Gardens. Food was my goal, but food was limited even in Coronation Market. We had no money, so we scraped and shared with friends. We were literally starving.

All the roads out of Kingston were blocked and riots were breaking out everywhere. We took shelter in a shack with a corrugated tin roof, belonging to Steve's brother. It was basically one room five meters square. A community of outhouses served as open-pit toilets with an open tap which served as a shower and source of fresh water. The water only came at certain times of the day, if at all. That toilet still fills my nightmares. It was the most disgusting place I have ever seen.

While we were living there I met Keisha, a local woman, and she became my friend. She brought drinks and helped me find food. Apart from Steve, she was the only companionship I had. She talked to me and took me in as if I were a close family friend. If it hadn't been for her, I don't think I would have survived.

Steve could manage to get to certain areas, but not others. Almost daily he would leave the shack and go out to visit his friends in the areas where he was allowed. There was no one for me to visit, and I was often left on my own.

When I did venture out it was terrifying. The people were out of control and a mob mentality had taken over. I have never witnessed violence on that level. While I was there I was in survival mode, every day. It is only with hindsight that I can appreciate the dangers I faced.

As luck would have it, I never left my home in the bush without my passport, so I had it with me in the shack. Somehow I managed to call the

UK and speak to a good friend called Delmar. His mother had a house in Jamaica, so he had first-hand knowledge of the violence and danger I was facing stuck in the middle of the revolt. Miraculously, he managed to purchase one of the last tickets out of the country.

I found that Amy and all my friends were watching the civil war unfold on the telly, and they were terrified for me. The Jamaican community in the UK was trying everything to understand the madness they were watching.

Getting out of Jamaica was the only answer. Not only did I leave all my belongings behind in my house, but I left my friends there. Steve was relieved for me to get out. He was my lover and my friend and knew that it was just too dangerous for me to stay. I worried for him and for all my friends. I felt as if I was abandoning them, leaving them to face a horrible situation on their own. It is a regret I still carry with me.

I managed to get a lift to the airport. It was Boxing Day in England, and my last day in Jamaica. I was wearing simple summer clothes and sandals on my feet and I was starving - my bones were sticking out. I was scared out of my mind.

Amy met me at Heathrow, and her eyes went wide with astonishment when she saw me walk through the doors. The bitter cold of Britain grabbed me and took its hold. It was freezing, and she held a coat out to me. I had no clothes, no shoes, no money and no job. I was, once again, as low as it gets.

Amy was visibly shocked at my appearance and could not take her eyes off my emaciated frame and the lost look in my eyes. She took me to a motel in Forest Gate, where Delmar paid for a room for a couple of days. I tried as best I could to regroup my thoughts and find the survival skills which had helped me through life.

What had happened in Jamaica was all over the TV. There was destruction everywhere. I was relieved to be out, but at the same time I was severely shocked at finding myself back in the UK. The feelings of guilt I had over deserting my friends was intense. England's cold and grey skies loomed over me. I was safe, but I was back in a country which was cold and controlled, and no longer felt like home. I still find it hard to grasp.

After a few days in the hotel I contacted a friend called Bob and asked if I could stay with him. I went to the local authority to apply for benefits, and was put into a YMCA - quite bizarre, considering that I had started my adult life in one. I had a sink, a shower and a small hotplate to cook on, so it was a mansion compared to my shack in the bush.

I got my benefits fortnightly and sent some money back to Steve in Jamaica. I felt a need to help him out. It took a while for me to realise that Britain was my life again. I had to process all that I had witnessed and left behind, and try and put it all to rest.

I still miss the warmth of Jamaica - not just the climate, but also the atmosphere. I miss the openness of the island. I miss swimming in the sea. I miss the lifestyle and the people. I would not trade my time there for anything. One day I hope to return, to see Keisha and all the rest of my friends. I know I will go back, but until then, I can only close my eyes and imagine that salty warm water on my skin.

CHAPTER NINE

Settling down

London was all a bit much for me. I needed a slower pace and more breathing space, so I contacted my friend Dave in Bristol and he offered to help. Through his connections, I found a small bedsit in Totterdown, just one room in grotty old house where I shared a kitchen and a toilet. Many of the other tenants were on the edge of society, with drug and drink problems.

To my surprise I discovered I had £500 in an account I hadn't known about, so I used the money to fly Steve to the UK. I wanted him to have a chance in life. He would have more opportunities here. Not all Jamaicans have birth certificates, but we managed to get him one and then we applied for his passport.

When he arrived at Heathrow, he was not immediately allowed through immigration. My friend Anna gave him an invitation, as all Jamaicans needed an official invitation to come to the UK. We waited three hours at the airport for him. When they finally let him through he was in a terrible mood, but he was safe and out of Jamaica.

It was a long bus journey from Heathrow back to Bristol and Steve's mood worsened with every mile. When he walked up the stairs to my little room, the landlord came out and had a word. Steve was not part of my rental agreement, so I was soon looking for different accommodation. When I had decided to buy the ticket for him, I had never truly thought about the reality of him being in the UK. All I wanted was for him to get away from the violence that was still smouldering and have some options in his life.

At first, Steve was amazed at the cleanliness of Britain. He tried to help my friend Dave with some building work, but the clients didn't want a big black Jamaican working on their property. Steve did not understand that it was overt racism. He wanted to work, and couldn't understand why he was denied at every turn. In Jamaica, he only ever mixed with his own class of people and never experienced racism. He now understands racism. After a while, he started to go to college to learn to read and write.

Amy had been working in London, but now she wanted to be closer to me so she came back to Bristol. London is a hard city for a young girl on her own, and Amy needed the change. It was now very cramped in the bedsit, so I went to the council, put my name on the list and got a two-bedroom place on Stapleton Road. We had no furniture, no possessions at all, but it was luxury in comparison to the bedsit and some of the places in Jamaica.

Steve was not working as he had no visa, and he could not find work on the black market. I took a series of jobs cleaning and caring for the elderly. Finally I found a job I liked and could care about, working in Stonebridge Park, a hostel for people with drug and alcohol addiction. It was a proper job with proper money, and I stayed there for two years.

Steve, on the other hand, was finding life in England tough. He wanted to work, but couldn't. He struggled to learn to read and write. And through it all I was supporting him. I even thought things would get better if we were married, so we tied the knot. It was not for a visa but for love.

Eventually he found a job at a dry cleaner's as a driver's mate, and things improved between us. But when he lost that job, our life quickly went wrong. He was living with me and off me, and he did nothing in the house; he would not clean or cook. In fact, when I came home for work, the flat was still messy and he spent the whole day playing video games. His moods became unbearable.

Amy's presence did not help matters. When she arrived from London she was not 'in a good place'. Neither was Steve. The two of them together were not a good mix. Amy is a very introverted person, but very honest and straightforward. If someone is going to stand up to anyone, it's Amy. She is loyal to a fault. She is very protective of me, and she didn't like the way Steve treated me. She let him know on many occasions how she felt about him living with me, taking and taking without giving back. In hindsight, I did agree with her and eventually I realised she was right, but at the time I wanted her to leave. It was all a bit much with her around. At least Steve was quiet and moody; Amy let herself be known.

To get Amy out of my house and into her own flat I had to declare her homeless. I described to the people at the council how aggressive the situation was with Steve and they found her a place almost immediately. Amy went to live in a hostel for a year.

Once she moved out, I realised that Steve was a huge part of the problem too. With the peace of mind I gained from Amy's absence in my home, I found the strength to ask him to leave, and I gave him a month to sort out a new place. He moved in with a friend from Jamaica, and my life was peaceful again.

Living on my own was bliss. I worked and saw friends and helped out Amy and Leon, who had now come back from Jamaica as there were no opportunities for him there. He was living on his own in Bristol and had a new girlfriend.

Steve was still a part of my life. I was the only one he trusted, and regardless of our living situation there was mutual respect between us. Whenever he had issues with paperwork or any business that involved reading and writing, I was the one he came to. At 52 I was finally on my own again, and I liked it.

I liked the work at Stonebridge Park. It was difficult, because it was shift work and included nights, but things in my life were calm. I made friends with a good group of women. I had spent so much time with Amy and Steve sorting out their problems that having time to myself was very refreshing.

Amy was better on her own in the hostel. I did worry about her, but she came to visit me regularly. Our relationship as mother and daughter was getting better. She was working at a pub and a garage. Her attitude towards most people was very negative, and she could still be very aggressive. Her mood swings were quite violent and I worried about her constantly. I would never let her live with me again, and that made neither of us happy. But her darkness had a profound effect on me.

My friends were not aware of Amy's problems and her aggression - or if they were, they never talked to me about them. But I longed to speak to someone about my daughter. As a mother, all I wanted was for her to be happy. It saddened me to know that she probably had never been truly happy. Maybe for a while in Jamaica we all had been, but that was fleeting and wasn't meant to last.

My child's depression seemed to me to be clinical, the result of some chemical imbalance in her brain. I wanted so much to pick her up and drive her to a doctor to have her tested, but she adamantly refused. I felt I could not discuss my fears with anyone, and her privacy was important to me. All a mother wants is for her children for to be happy.

Working nights at the hostel began to take its toll on me, but I did enjoy working hands-on in a care capacity so I found another job without the long nights. The Salvation Army hired me as a resettlement and tenancy sustainment worker, helping to resettle homeless people and those coming out of care into society again. I was over the moon about this job. It was such a nice environment there – the people I worked with were lovely and I did not have to work nights or weekends. To make it all perfect, it was just up the road.

I stayed for four years. At any one time I would have eight to ten clients. Basically, I helped them to leave their Salvation Army or other hostel and move into a council property. The hardest part of my job started after they were settled. Keeping people straight, clean and sane in the mundanity of day-to-day life is a difficult thing indeed. Most of my clients were used to the ups and downs of life on the street, with drug-induced highs and alcohol-fuelled lows. Getting them to live a 'normal' life' was the trick. Besides helping them to organise their lives, I had to make sure they kept on living them.

Usually I was alone in the community with just my mobile phone. It was safe, but sometimes I did have to help out a service user who was violent. You never knew who or what was going to appear on the other side of a door when you knocked on it.

Many of my service users were addicts and alcoholics. When their benefits came in, I went with them to the Post Office to get their money. I wanted to ensure they used it for bills and not to get high. Angry and violent 'friends' who always seemed to show up on the days my clients got their benefit money were some of the worst. I had to make sure my clients paid their bills, and if they hadn't I had to sort it out. There were neighbour disputes and relapses into drug use, fights and disappearances. I would call ambulances and visit them in hospital. If they got better I would help them find courses to attend which would help them to stay better.

My clients were not evil people, they were just vulnerable. I was a soldier on the front line. I know the realities of the benefit culture. Even though the job involved mounds of paperwork, risk assessments, government stats and bureaucratic reports, I loved it.

I realise now that I was fascinated with the clients' stories. I wanted to know what had made them choose a life of crime, drugs and alcohol. How was I so different from them? What was it that had put me on the opposite side of the desk? Most of the time, when I heard their stories of their childhood, it was no worse than mine had been. I identified with their anger. I know what isolation feels like. I have walked in their shoes – it was what made me so good in my job.

After four years of working on the front line, I was burnt out. I became very ill with the stress of it all. I also needed to move house, because some of my clients had become my neighbours. Seeing them outside a work environment was too much to handle - I had given myself away. My depression came down as before, like a black cloud raining down on me.

This time though, I sought help. My doctor prescribed some anti-depressants and put me on long-term sick leave. Looking back, I realise now that I should have sought medical attention at other times in my life when that darkness had descended on me. I never went back to work at the Salvation Army – It had taken too heavy a toll.

After the pills were prescribed, I needed to rest and recuperate. It was during this time that I began to write, and poetry was flowing on to the page.

I spent many a night staring at the moon and putting to the page whatever came to me.

I also started to feel the need to tell my story. I wanted to get it all out. I had never talked to anyone about my time in care at Barnardo's, and now it needed to be released.

There were so many fears about my past that needed to be faced. One way I managed to confront them was to get into public speaking. Specifically, I addressed people who worked in care. By speaking directly of my time in care and what it was like for me, I released the demons of my past - not all of them, but some.

Leon, my beautiful son, was suffering too. His relationship with his girlfriend was chaotic and unhealthy from the beginning. Eventually the love soured. After three and a half years of trying to live together and make it work, he split up, very dramatically, with his partner. The break-up left one innocent victim, my granddaughter Aaliyah.

My own gene pool is a mystery, but my future gene pool is right in front of me, a future for me, through me. It cannot be taken away. My children are my children and my granddaughter is my granddaughter. Nobody can change that. When I look into Aaliyah's eyes I can see my future and my past. There is no stronger bond. I have to thank my son for his gift.

Until the friend I made at the YMCA came along, I had never spoken to another black person. I wonder how I would have turned out if Barnardo's had recognised my need for a mentor. Would I feel more confident of my skin, would I be raising my head just a little higher? I wish someone could have prepared me and told me what it was like to be the victim of prejudice. There was no one to tell me how to do my hair, or how to care for my skin. It wasn't until I became a grown woman that I learned about the effects of using cocoa butter on black skin, or black hair products. The matrons at Barnardo's thought I had severe eczema because I had white patches on my skin, a condition many bi-racial people experience. Barnardo's met my basic care needs, but my heart and mind were left to their own devices.

Now, it is easy being black. It is easy because no one stares at me intensely when I walk into a shop or a pub. No one follows me around stores waiting for me to shoplift. No one gets up from their seat on a bus when I sit next to them. But I do stay away from places where there are no other black people. Maybe this is a product of my age and my experience? The black people of my generation paved the way for the black people today. Young black people today have no idea of the horrifying experience we went through just so that our descendants can stay at a hotel with white people, or walk into a restaurant. There still is a massive wave of racism in this country. People still get rejected because of the colour of their skin, but at least now there are established government bodies and legal entities to go to and scream to when it happens. They are so much better protected that I was. And they have many more opportunities.

It does make me angry that a lot of the black youth of today have no form of respect, regardless of their skin colour. I shudder to think what would have happened to me if I had acted the way I see them act. I kept my mouth shut and went on with my business. Black kids today do not know how much freedom they have. They have the freedom to be mouthy, to give attitude, to call the racist card. And even though sometimes I want to explain what respect really is, I don't. It is good enough to know that I helped to make the path free and clear for them. Back in my day, you fought alone. When I see older black people being cajoled by the youngsters to take a stand, I want to say 'Stop! They fought hard for you and now they are tired.'

Thanks to the fight against racial discrimination, white people today have no choice but to accept us and work alongside with us. Mixed-race marriage has changed the way white people of the older generation have to act. Their children are having children with black partners, so their grandchildren are bi-racial, dual heritage, mixed race - whatever you want to call it. Sometimes, when I am at the park with my granddaughter, I see other grandparents, white people, with grandchildren who are black like me. I laugh, knowing that 20 years ago the same couple would have crossed to the other side of the street so as not to walk next to the likes of me.

I knew I was adopted, but I didn't know what it meant. Dad never made a big show about it, nor did he once say anything about me being black. I think because he was working class and accepted me, everyone else in our community accepted me. I was his, and that made me a part of our community.

The need to know your ancestry seems to be a recent phenomenon. When I was growing up, it didn't seem to be an issue. Even in Barnardo's I had yet to actually grasp what it meant to be adopted. My father was all I had ever known - he was my family. It didn't occur to me that he didn't have black skin or that we didn't look alike. He was just my dad.

It was after he had died and I left Barnardo's that the questions came. I wanted to answer them, but I couldn't. People need to put you in a box, and I had no idea what to say. By the time I hit my twenties it was really hard. I was becoming completely self-aware, but I had nothing to be aware of. My history was in an institution. Before that, a loving, kind man had been taken away from me. I now know that he knew the truth about my birth mother. I know he knew her and maybe, just maybe, he knew about my birth father. He could have told me my mother's name and helped me to find out more about my brother and sisters, but he died before I was ready to ask him and before he was ready to tell me. I will never know.

It was a massive loss in so many ways. As I look back now, I scream out the questions. Why didn't anyone else think to ask on my behalf? No one at Barnardo's took an interest. None of the social workers who were checking up on me cared enough to ask. What about Janet? No one who was 'caring' for me ever thought to ask him about the truth of my birth. Didn't they think I would want to know?

Things really came to a head for me when I started to mix with the Afro-Caribbean Community. They assumed I too was Afro-Caribbean. Of course I am not, but back then I needed to belong so badly that I would have said I was anything.

The first time I was surrounded by black people I was in my mid thirties. For all those years I had been trying to get by in a white world. It was not until after I had had children and got divorced that I finally got to know other people with black skin.

One day I was in a shoe shop when I realised that I and another black woman were being followed by an assistant, who thought we might be stealing. The other woman looked at me and I looked at her and we both said 'They are following us, aren't they?' That's how I met Beverly.

She invited me to a Jamaican Independence Day celebration on Salisbury Plain, and that invitation was just what I needed at that point in my life. We got dressed up and boarded a coach full of Jamaican people. I was amazed. We arrived at a huge army hall and, as we walked in, my coat was taken by a white man. A white man! The hall was full of Jamaican soldiers, hundreds of them. Beverly's brother was a soldier, which was why she had been invited.

That night was a 'first' for many things for me. The Jamaican soldiers were being served by white soldiers in honour of their service to the crown - I had never seen black people being waited on by white people. The Afro-Caribbean food was delicious, and the band made me want to dance all night. The black voices were music to my ears, and all I wanted to do was sit and chat all night.

Chillin' in this room
I like being in a room where everyone is black.

I just sit back in my chair

I can really relax

I like being in a room where everyone is black

It is one of those times when I don't feel under attack

I like being in a room where I can laugh and be loud

Where people don't judge me as being one of those in a crowd

I like being in this room talking to you

I like being black

I like being like you.

That night I felt as if I was the lead actor in the play of my life, and the lines were all mine. As an actor in my own play, I could mould the drama to my whims. 'Yes, I'm from Jamaica. Sadly, my mother is dead; I never knew my father.'

The real Anna was hidden deep inside, and she hated talking about her unknown self. Afro-Caribbean people are far more accepting, because they have all been separated from family at one time or another. They believed me when I said I was Jamaican. It was the first time I had been embarrassed about my past and done something about it. It felt good to be a part of something, even if I was lying. But a voice inside kept saying, it might be true. Your father might have been of Jamaican descent.

Back on the coach, after the party, Beverley asked why I was so quiet. And if I am honest with myself, I can see the truth falling on my shoulders like heavy snow. I could not share with her my deep shame of not knowing my ancestry. Why was I black? Who gave me this skin? I knew my mother was white, but who was my father? Everyone at the party knew one another; they had cousins or family or neighbours that linked them all. My made-up self became a part of that chain, but the real me was an unconnected link. I desperately wanted to be a part of the chain.

That night brought a new awareness as well. Not only was it the first time I had socialised with black men, I also realised I was very attracted to them. After that night, there was no going back. I no longer wanted to be a token black woman on the arm of a white man. I discovered that black men have the same skin as me. They have the same kind of hair. We like the same music and the same food. They can dance! And, we laugh about the same things. Afro-Caribbean men don't get stressed over the little things in life. If a white man said to me 'You have beautiful skin', it meant my skin was beautiful because it was black, but when a black man says it, it is because my skin is beautiful – full stop. That night made me realise that being with a black man was the best thing I could do to be more like 'me' in my black skin.

Yes - I have been the victim of out-and-out racism in the street. But it is the underhanded racism I find the hardest to deal with. Being called a nigger in the street is much easier to take than white people who befriend you so they can have a black friend. Liberal, educated middle-class white people who can't wait to tell you that they have adopted a black child, or that they marched 'for us'. They were our 'friends'. Then, they say things like, 'You are so different from the blacks on TV.' I was never invited round to dinner on a random Friday night just to catch up with my white friends. My invitations always seemed to be orchestrated - I was a 'token' black friend.

One would think the working-class whites would be the worst, but they aren't. When they marched for rights at work, they marched for all of us. When they shouted 'nigger' in my face, I knew the truth. They will never invite me to dinner, but we have a common cause. And I respect that. It's the liberal middle classes trying their hardest to befriend me because I am black that make me the angriest.

In my personal relationships, I can honestly say that my ex-husband Charles never made me feel like his 'token' black girl. He accepted me as me. He didn't see my skin as an issue or a non-issue. His sister adopted two black girls. Charles was exposed to the idea of mixed race families. Mary never made it much of an issue - she just got on with being a mother to her girls.

I know I will never know the true genetic origin of my skin, and for that I will always feel regret. But I have made my way in the world by surviving. I believe that the origins of my strength in the face of all the prejudice I have endured lie in my black relatives shouting out from my past: "Be proud, you are one of us."

POSTSCRIPT

The day I was placed in Barnardo's was a fateful day, but it was my fate. I know there were powers at work around me guiding me to that place, but it was my place to have. I know now after working with people who live on the fringes of society that something made me different. My life could have been filled with substance abuse, violence, even prison. But each time my darkness came, I found some light. Something inside me made me seek something greater. And I know that that something was my father's love.

The first seven years of my life were filled with the warmth of a family. That warmth lets me look into the eyes of my children and see love. I look into my granddaughter's eyes and see love. I look at them, and I see me. They are who I am.

———